Romeo and Juliet

CORINNE J. NADEN

INTRODUCTION BY JOSEPH SOBRAN

m̖c Marshall Cavendish
Benchmark
New York

Series consultant: Richard Larkin

Marshall Cavendish
99 White Plains Road
Tarrytown, New York 10591
www.marshallcavendish.us

Library of Congress Cataloging-in-Publication Data
Naden, Corinne J.
Romeo and Juliet / by Corinne J. Naden.
p. cm. — (Shakespeare explained)
Summary: "A literary analysis of the play Romeo and Juliet. Includes
information on the history and culture of Elizabethan England"—Provided by publisher.
Includes bibliographical references and index.
ISBN 978-0-7614-3031-5
1. Shakespeare, William, 1564-1616. Romeo and Juliet—Juvenile literature.
2. Romeo (Fictitious character)—Juvenile literature. 3. Juliet
(Fictitious character)—Juvenile literature. I. Title.
PR2831.N33 2009
822.3'3—dc22
2008014407

Photo research by: Linda Sykes
Elliott Franks/Wireimage: front cover; Michael Caven/istockphoto: back cover, 8, 25; ©Michael
Braun/iStockphoto: 1; ©Marco Manzini/iStockphoto: 1; Neven Mendrila/Shutterstock: 3; Raciro/
istockphoto: 4; Art Parts RF: 6, 13, 24, 32; ©Nik Wheeler/Corbis: 11; Portraitgalerie, Schloss Ambras,
Inssbruck, Austria/Erich Lessing/Art Resource, NY: 18; AA World Travel Library/Alamy: 20; ©Hideo
Kurihara/Alamy: 22; ©Corbis Sygma: 27; ©Andrew Fox/Corbis: 30; Mikhall/Shutterstock: 36-37; The
Everett Collection: 37 left; Neven Mendrila/Shutterstock: 37 right; Visuals Arts Library, London/
Alamy: 41; The Everett Collection: 43, 75; Royal Shakespeare Company: 50; ©Sara Krulwich/ New
York Times Pictures/ Redux: 53; Royal Shakespeare Company: 57; ©Tristram Kenton/ Lebrecht
Music and Arts: 62; Mary Evans Picture Library/Everett Collection: 64; Southampton City Art Gallery,
Hampshire UK/Bridgeman Art Gallery: 71; The Kobal Collection: 85; Photofest : 93; Gjon Mili/Time
and Life Pictures/Getty Images: 112.

Editor: Deborah Grahame
Publisher: Michelle Bisson
Art Director: Anahid Hamparian
Series Design: Kay Petronio

Printed in Malaysia
135642

Contents

Shakespeare and His World

WILLIAM SHAKESPEARE,

OFTEN NICKNAMED "THE BARD," IS, BEYOND ANY COMPARISON, THE MOST TOWERING NAME IN ENGLISH LITERATURE. MANY CONSIDER HIS PLAYS THE GREATEST EVER WRITTEN. HE STANDS OUT EVEN AMONG GENIUSES.

Yet the Bard is also closer to our hearts than lesser writers, and his tremendous reputation should neither intimidate us nor prevent us from enjoying the simple delights he offers in such abundance. It is as if he had written for each of us personally. As he himself put it, "One touch of nature makes the whole world kin."

Such tragedies as *Hamlet*, *Romeo and Juliet*, and *Macbeth* are world-famous, still performed on stage and in films. These and others have also been adapted for radio, television, opera, ballet, pantomime, novels, comic books, and other media. Two of the best ways to become familiar with them are to watch some of the many fine movies that have been made of them and to listen to recordings of them by some of the world's great actors.

Even Shakespeare's individual characters have a life of their own, like real historical figures. Hamlet is still regarded as the most challenging role ever written for an actor. Roughly as many whole books have been written about Hamlet, an imaginary character, as about actual historical figures such as Abraham Lincoln and Napoleon Bonaparte.

Shakespeare created an amazing variety of vivid characters. One of Shakespeare's most peculiar traits was that he loved his characters so much—even some of his villains and secondary or comic characters—that at times he let them run away with the play, stealing attention from his heroes and heroines.

So in *A Midsummer Night's Dream* audiences remember the absurd and lovable fool Bottom the Weaver better than the lovers who are the main characters. Romeo's friend Mercutio is more fiery and witty than Romeo himself; legend claims that Shakespeare said he had to kill Mercutio or Mercutio would have killed the play.

Shakespeare also wrote dozens of comedies and historical plays, as well as nondramatic poems. Although his tragedies are now regarded as his greatest works, he freely mixed them with comedy and history. And his sonnets are among the supreme love poems in the English language.

It is Shakespeare's mastery of the English language that keeps his words familiar to us today. Every literate person knows dramatic lines such as "Wherefore art thou Romeo?"; "My kingdom for a horse!"; "To be or not to be: that is the question"; "Friends, Romans, countrymen, lend me your ears"; and "What fools these mortals be!" Shakespeare's sonnets are noted for their sweetness: "Shall I compare thee to a summer's day?"

A PAIR OF STAR-CROSS'D LOVERS

SHAKESPEARE'S LANGUAGE

WITHOUT A DOUBT, SHAKESPEARE WAS THE GREATEST MASTER OF THE ENGLISH LANGUAGE WHO EVER LIVED. BUT JUST WHAT DOES THAT MEAN?

Shakespeare's vocabulary was huge, full of references to the Bible as well as Greek and Roman mythology. Yet his most brilliant phrases often combine very simple and familiar words:

"WHAT'S IN A NAME? THAT WHICH WE CALL A ROSE BY ANY OTHER NAME WOULD SMELL AS SWEET."

He has delighted countless millions of readers. And we know him only through his language. He has shaped modern English far more than any other writer.

Or, to put it in more personal terms, you probably quote his words several times every day without realizing it, even if you have never suspected that Shakespeare could be a source of pleasure to you.

So why do so many English-speaking readers find his language so difficult? It is our language, too, but it has changed so much that it is no longer quite the same language—nor a completely different one, either.

Shakespeare's English and ours overlap without being identical. He would have some difficulty understanding us, too! Many of our everyday words and phrases would baffle him.

Shakespeare, for example, would not know what we meant by a *car,* a *radio,* a *movie,* a *television,* a *computer,* or a *sitcom,* since these things did not even exist in his time. Our old-fashioned term *railroad train,* would be unimaginable to him, far in the distant future. We would have to explain to him (if we could) what *nuclear weapons, electricity,* and *democracy* are. He would also be a little puzzled by common expressions such as *high-tech, feel the heat, approval ratings, war criminal, judgmental,* and *whoopie cushion.*

So how can we call him "the greatest master of the English language"? It might seem as if he barely spoke English at all! (He would, however, recognize much of our dirty slang, even if he pronounced it slightly differently. His plays also contain many racial insults to Jews, Africans, Italians, Irish, and others. Today he would be called "insensitive.")

Many of the words of Shakespeare's time have become archaic. Words like *thou, thee, thy, thyself,* and *thine,* which were among the most common words in the language in Shakespeare's day, have all but disappeared today. We simply say *you* for both singular and plural, formal and familiar. Most other modern languages have kept their *thou.*

Sometimes the same words now have different meanings. We are apt to be misled by such simple, familiar words as *kind, wonderful, waste, just,* and *dear,* which he often uses in ways that differ from our usage.

Shakespeare also doesn't always use the words we expect to hear, the words that we ourselves would naturally use. When we might automatically say, "I beg your pardon" or just "Sorry," he might say, "I cry you mercy."

Often a glossary and footnotes will solve all three of these problems for us. But it is most important to bear in mind that Shakespeare was often hard for his first audiences to understand. Even in his own time his rich language was challenging. And this was deliberate. Shakespeare was inventing his own kind of English. It remains unique today.

A child doesn't learn to talk by using a dictionary. Children learn first by sheer immersion. We teach babies by pointing at things and saying their names. Yet the toddler always learns faster than we can teach! Even as babies we are geniuses. Dictionaries can help us later, when we already speak and read the language well (and learn more slowly).

So the best way to learn Shakespeare is not to depend on the footnotes and glossary too much, but instead to be like a baby: just get into the flow of the language. Go to performances of the plays or watch movies of them.

THE LANGUAGE HAS A MAGICAL WAY OF TEACHING ITSELF, IF WE LET IT. THERE IS NO REASON TO FEEL STUPID OR FRUSTRATED WHEN IT DOESN'T COME EASILY.

Hundreds of phrases have entered the English language from *Hamlet* alone, including "to hold, as t'were, the mirror up to nature"; "murder most foul"; "the thousand natural shocks that flesh is heir to"; "flaming youth"; "a countenance more in sorrow than in anger"; "the play's the thing"; "neither a borrower nor a lender be"; "in my mind's eye"; "something is rotten in the state of Denmark"; "alas, poor Yorick"; and "the lady doth protest too much, methinks."

From other plays we get the phrases "star-crossed lovers"; "what's in a name?"; "we have scotched the snake, not killed it"; "one fell swoop"; "it was Greek to me;" "I come to bury Caesar, not to praise him"; and "the most unkindest cut of all"—all these are among our household words. In fact, Shakespeare even gave us the expression "household words." No wonder his contemporaries marveled at his "fine filed phrase" and swooned at the "mellifluous and honey-tongued Shakespeare."

Shakespeare's words seem to combine music, magic, wisdom, and humor:

"THE COURSE OF TRUE LOVE NEVER DID RUN SMOOTH."

"HE JESTS AT SCARS THAT NEVER FELT A WOUND."

"THE FAULT, DEAR BRUTUS, IS NOT IN OUR STARS, BUT IN OURSELVES, THAT WE ARE UNDERLINGS."

"COWARDS DIE MANY TIMES BEFORE THEIR DEATHS; THE VALIANT NEVER TASTE OF DEATH BUT ONCE."

"NOT THAT I LOVED CAESAR LESS, BUT THAT I LOVED ROME MORE."

THERE ARE MORE THINGS IN HEAVEN AND EARTH, HORATIO, THAN ARE DREAMT OF IN YOUR PHILOSOPHY."

"BREVITY IS THE SOUL OF WIT."

"THERE'S A DIVINITY THAT SHAPES OUR ENDS, ROUGH-HEW THEM HOW WE WILL."

Four centuries after Shakespeare lived, to speak English is to quote him. His huge vocabulary and linguistic fertility are still astonishing. He has had a powerful effect on all of us, whether we realize it or not. We may wonder how it is even possible for a single human being to say so many memorable things.

Only the King James translation of the Bible, perhaps, has had a more profound and pervasive influence on the English language than Shakespeare. And, of course, the Bible was written by many authors over many centuries, and the King James translation, published in 1611, was the combined effort of many scholars.

EARLY LIFE

So who, exactly, was Shakespeare? Mystery surrounds his life, largely because few records were kept during his time. Some people have even doubted his identity, arguing that the real author of Shakespeare's plays must have been a man of superior formal education and wide experience. In a sense such doubts are a natural and understandable reaction to his rare, almost miraculous powers of expression, but some people feel that the doubts themselves show a lack of respect for the supremely human poet.

Most scholars agree that Shakespeare was born in the town of Stratford-upon-Avon in the county of Warwickshire, England, in April 1564. He was baptized, according to local church records, Gulielmus (William) Shakspere (the name was spelled in several different ways) on April 26 of that year. He was one of several children, most of whom died young.

His father, John Shakespeare (or Shakspere), was a glove maker and, at times, a town official. He was often in debt or being fined for unknown delinquencies, perhaps failure to attend church regularly. It is suspected that John was a "recusant" (secret and illegal) Catholic, but there is no proof. Many

scholars have found Catholic tendencies in Shakespeare's plays, but whether Shakespeare was Catholic or not we can only guess.

At the time of Shakespeare's birth, England was torn by religious controversy and persecution. The country had left the Roman Catholic Church during the reign of King Henry VIII, who had died in 1547. Two of Henry's children, Edward and Mary, ruled after his death. When his daughter Elizabeth I became queen in 1558, she upheld his claim that the monarch of England was also head of the English Church.

Did William attend the local grammar school? He was probably entitled to, given his father's prominence in Stratford, but again, we face a frustrating absence of proof, and many people of the time learned to read very well without schooling. If he went to the town school, he would also have learned the rudiments of Latin.

We know very little about the first half of William's life. In 1582, when he was eighteen, he married Anne Hathaway, eight years his senior. Their first daughter, Susanna, was born six months later. The following year they had twins, Hamnet and Judith.

At this point William disappears from the records again. By the early 1590s we find "William Shakespeare" in London, a member of the city's leading acting company, called the Lord Chamberlain's Men. Many of Shakespeare's greatest roles, we are told, were first performed by the company's star, Richard Burbage.

Curiously, the first work published under (and identified with) Shakespeare's name was not a play but a long erotic poem, *Venus and Adonis*, in 1593. It was dedicated to the young Earl of Southampton, Henry Wriothesley.

Venus and Adonis was a spectacular success, and Shakespeare was immediately hailed as a major poet. In 1594 he dedicated a longer, more serious poem to Southampton, *The Rape of Lucrece*. It was another hit, and for many years, these two poems were considered Shakespeare's greatest works, despite the popularity of his plays.

"A ROSE BY ANY OTHER NAME"

TODAY MOVIES, NOT LIVE PLAYS, ARE THE MORE POPULAR ART FORM. FORTUNATELY MOST OF SHAKESPEARE'S PLAYS HAVE BEEN FILMED, AND THE BEST OF THESE MOVIES OFFER AN EXCELLENT WAY TO MAKE THE BARD'S ACQUAINTANCE. RECENTLY, KENNETH BRANAGH HAS BECOME A RESPECTED CONVERTER OF SHAKESPEARE'S PLAYS INTO FILM.

Hamlet

Hamlet, Shakespeare's most famous play, has been well filmed several times. In 1948 Laurence Olivier won three Academy Awards—for best picture, best actor, and best director—for his version of the play. The film allowed him to show some of the magnetism that made him famous on the stage. Nobody spoke Shakespeare's lines more thrillingly.

The young Derek Jacobi played Hamlet in a 1980 BBC production of the play, with Patrick Stewart (now best known for *Star Trek, the Next Generation*) as the guilty king. Jacobi, like Olivier, has a gift for speaking the lines freshly; he never seems to be merely reciting the famous and familiar words. But whereas Olivier has animal passion, Jacobi is more intellectual. It is fascinating to compare the ways these two outstanding actors play Shakespeare's most complex character.

Franco Zeffirelli's 1990 *Hamlet*, starring Mel Gibson, is fascinating in a different way. Gibson, of course, is best known as an action hero, and he is not well suited to this supremely witty and introspective role, but Zeffirelli cuts the text drastically, and the result turns *Hamlet* into something that few people would have expected: a short, swift-moving action movie. Several of the other characters are brilliantly played.

Henry IV, Part One

The 1979 BBC Shakespeare series production does a commendable job in this straightforward approach to the play. Battle scenes are effective despite obvious restrictions in an indoor studio setting. Anthony Quayle gives jovial Falstaff a darker edge, and Tim Pigott-Smith's Hotspur is buoyed by some humor. Jon Finch plays King Henry IV with noble authority, and David Gwillim gives Hal a surprisingly successful transformation from boy prince to heir apparent.

Julius Caesar

No really good movie of *Julius Caesar* exists, but the 1953 film, with Marlon Brando as Mark Antony, will do. James Mason is a thoughtful Brutus, and John Gielgud, then ranked with Laurence Olivier among the greatest Shakespearean actors, plays the villainous Cassius. The film is rather dull, and Brando is out of place in a Roman toga, but it is still worth viewing.

Macbeth

Roman Polanski is best known as a director of thrillers and horror films, so it may seem natural that he should have done his 1971 *The Tragedy of Macbeth* as an often-gruesome slasher flick. But this is also one of the most vigorous of all Shakespeare films. Macbeth and his wife are played by Jon Finch and Francesca Annis, neither known for playing Shakespeare, but they are young and attractive in roles that are usually given to older actors, which gives the story a fresh flavor.

The Merchant of Venice

Once again the matchless Sir Laurence Olivier delivers a great performance as Shylock with his wife Joan Plowright as Portia in the 1974 TV film, adapted from the 1970 National Theater (of Britain) production. A 1980 BBC offering features Warren Mitchell as Shylock and Gemma Jones as Portia, with John Rhys-Davies as Salerio. The most recent production, starring Al Pacino as Shylock, Jeremy Irons as Antonio, and Joseph Fiennes as Bassanio, was filmed in Venice and released in 2004.

A Midsummer Night's Dream

Because of the prestige of his tragedies, we tend to forget how many comedies Shakespeare wrote—nearly twice the number of tragedies. Of these perhaps the most popular has always been the enchanting, atmospheric, and very silly masterpiece *A Midsummer Night's Dream*.

In more recent times several films have been made of *A Midsummer Night's Dream*. Among the more notable have been Max Reinhardt's 1935 black-and-white version, with Mickey Rooney (then a child star) as Puck.

Of the several film versions, the one starring Kevin Kline as Bottom and Stanley Tucci as Puck, made in 1999 with nineteenth-century costumes and directed by Michael Hoffman, ranks among the finest, and is surely one of the most sumptuous to watch.

Othello

Orson Welles did a budget European version in 1952, now available as a restored DVD. Laurence Olivier's 1965 film performance is predictably remarkable, though it has been said that he would only approach the part by honoring, even emulating, Paul Robeson's definitive interpretation that ran on Broadway in 1943. (Robeson was the first black actor to play Othello, the Moor of Venice, and he did so to critical acclaim, though sadly his performance was never filmed.) Maggie Smith plays a formidable Desdemona opposite Olivier, and her youth and energy will surprise younger audiences who know her only from the Harry Potter films. Laurence Fishburne brilliantly portrayed Othello in the 1995 film, costarring with Kenneth Branagh as a surprisingly human Iago, though Irène Jacob's Desdemona was disappointingly weak.

Romeo and Juliet

This, the world's most famous love story, has been filmed many times, twice very successfully over the last generation. Franco Zeffirelli directed a hit version in 1968 with Leonard Whiting and the rapturously pretty Olivia Hussey, set in Renaissance Italy. Baz Luhrmann made a much more contemporary version, with a loud rock score, starring Leonardo Di Caprio and Claire Danes, in 1996.

It seems safe to say that Shakespeare would have preferred Zeffirelli's movie, with its superior acting and rich, romantic, sun-drenched Italian scenery.

The Tempest

A 1960 Hallmark Hall of Fame production featured Maurice Evans as Prospero, Lee Remick as Miranda, Roddy McDowall as Ariel, and Richard Burton as Caliban. The special effects are primitive and the costumes are ludicrous, but it moves along at a fast pace. Another TV version aired in 1998 and was nominated for a Golden Globe. Peter Fonda played Gideon Prosper, and Katherine Heigl played his daughter Miranda Prosper. Sci-Fi fans may already know that the classic 1956 film *Forbidden Planet* is modeled on themes and characters from the play.

Twelfth Night

Trevor Nunn adapted the play for the 1996 film he also directed in a rapturous Edwardian setting, with big names like Helena Bonham Carter, Richard E. Grant, Imogen Stubbs, and Ben Kingsley as Feste. A 2003 film set in modern Britain provides an interesting multicultural experience; it features an Anglo-Indian cast with Parminder Nagra (*Bend It Like Beckham*) playing Viola. For the truly intrepid, a twelve-minute silent film made in 1910 does a fine job of capturing the play through visual gags and over-the-top gesturing.

THESE FILMS HAVE BEEN SELECTED FOR SEVERAL QUALITIES: APPEAL AND ACCESSIBILITY TO MODERN AUDIENCES, EXCELLENCE IN ACTING, PACING, VISUAL BEAUTY, AND, OF COURSE, FIDELITY TO SHAKESPEARE. THEY ARE THE MOTION PICTURES WE JUDGE MOST LIKELY TO HELP STUDENTS UNDERSTAND THE SOURCE OF THE BARD'S LASTING POWER.

SHAKESPEARE'S THEATER

Today we sometimes speak of "live entertainment." In Shakespeare's day, of course, all entertainment was live, because recordings, films, television, and radio did not yet exist. Even printed books were a novelty.

In fact, most communication in those days was difficult. Transportation was not only difficult but slow, chiefly by horse and boat. Most people were illiterate peasants who lived on farms that they seldom left; cities grew up along waterways and were subject to frequent plagues that could wipe out much of the population within weeks.

Money—in coin form, not paper—was scarce and hardly existed outside the cities. By today's standards, even the rich were poor. Life was precarious. Most children died young, and famine or disease might kill anyone at any time. Everyone was familiar with death. Starvation was not rare or remote, as it is to most of us today. Medical care was poor and might kill as many people as it healed.

ELIZABETH I, A GREAT PATRON OF POETRY AND THE THEATER, WROTE SONNETS AND TRANSLATED CLASSIC WORKS.

This was the grim background of Shakespeare's theater during the reign of Queen Elizabeth I, who ruled from 1558 until her death in 1603. During that period England was also torn by religious conflict, often violent, among Roman Catholics who were loyal to the Pope, adherents of the Church of England who were loyal to the queen, and the Puritans who would take over the country in the revolution of 1642.

Under these conditions, most forms of entertainment were luxuries that were out of most people's reach. The only way to hear music was to be in the actual physical presence of singers or musicians with their instruments, which were primitive by our standards.

One brutal form of entertainment, popular in London, was bear-baiting. A bear was blinded and chained to a stake, where fierce dogs called mastiffs were turned loose to tear him apart. The theaters had to compete with the bear gardens, as they were called, for spectators.

The Puritans, or radical Protestants, objected to bear-baiting and tried to ban it. Despite their modern reputation, the Puritans were anything but conservative. Conservative people, attached to old customs, hated them. They seemed to upset everything. (Many of America's first settlers, such as the Pilgrims who came over on the *Mayflower*, were dissidents who were fleeing the Church of England.)

Plays were extremely popular, but they were primitive, too. They had to be performed outdoors in the afternoon because of the lack of indoor lighting. Often the "theater" was only an enclosed courtyard. Probably the versions of Shakespeare's plays that we know today were not used in full, but shortened to about two hours for actual performance.

But eventually more regular theaters were built, featuring a raised stage extending into the audience. Poorer spectators (illiterate "groundlings") stood on the ground around it, at times exposed to rain and snow. Wealthier people sat in raised tiers above. Aside from some costumes, there were few props or special effects and almost no scenery. Much had to be imagined: Whole battles might be represented by a few actors with swords. Thunder might be simulated by rattling a sheet of tin offstage.

The plays were far from realistic and, under the conditions of the time, could hardly try to be. Above the rear of the main stage was a small balcony. (It was this balcony from which Juliet spoke to Romeo.) Ghosts and witches might appear by entering through a trapdoor in the stage floor.

Unlike the modern theater, Shakespeare's Globe Theater—he describes it as "this wooden O"—had no curtain separating the stage from the audience. This allowed intimacy between the players and the spectators.

THE RECONSTRUCTED GLOBE THEATER WAS COMPLETED IN 1997 AND IS LOCATED IN LONDON, JUST 200 YARDS (183 METERS) FROM THE SITE OF THE ORIGINAL.

"A PLAGUE O' BOTH YOUR HOUSES!"

The spectators probably reacted rowdily to the play, not listening in reverent silence. After all they had come to have fun! And few of them were scholars. Again, a play had to amuse people who could not read.

The lines of plays were written and spoken in prose or, more often, in a form of verse called iambic pentameter (ten syllables with five stresses per line). There was no attempt at modern realism. Only males were allowed on the stage, so some of the greatest women's roles ever written had to be played by boys or men. (The same is true, by the way, of the ancient Greek theater.)

Actors had to be versatile, skilled not only in acting, but also in fencing, singing, dancing, and acrobatics. Within its limitations, the theater offered a considerable variety of spectacles.

Plays were big business, not yet regarded as high art, sponsored by important and powerful people (the queen loved them as much as the groundlings did). The London acting companies also toured and performed in the provinces. When plagues struck London, the government might order the theaters to be closed to prevent the spread of disease among crowds. (They remained empty for nearly two years from 1593 to 1594.)

As the theater became more popular, the Puritans grew as hostile to it as they were to bear-baiting. Plays, like books, were censored by the government, and the Puritans fought to increase restrictions, eventually banning any mention of God and other sacred topics on the stage.

In 1642 the Puritans shut down all the theaters in London, and in 1644 they had the Globe demolished. The theaters remained closed until Charles's son King Charles II was restored to the throne in 1660 and the hated Puritans were finally vanquished.

But, by then, the tradition of Shakespeare's theater had been fatally interrupted. His plays remained popular, but they were often rewritten by inferior dramatists and it was many years before they were performed (again) as he had originally written them.

THE ROYAL SHAKESPEARE THEATER, IN STRATFORD-UPON-AVON, WAS CLOSED IN 2007. A NEWLY DESIGNED INTERIOR WITH A 1000-SEAT AUDITORIUM WILL BE COMPLETED IN 2010.

Today, of course, the plays are performed both in theaters and in films, sometimes in costumes of the period (ancient Rome for *Julius Caesar*, medieval England for *Henry V*), sometimes in modern dress (*Richard III* has recently been reset in England in the 1930s).

PLAYS

In the England of Queen Elizabeth I, plays were enjoyed by all classes of people, but they were not yet respected as a serious form of art.

Shakespeare's plays began to appear in print in individual, or "quarto," editions in 1594, but none of these bore his name until 1598. Although his tragedies are now ranked as his supreme achievements, his name was first associated with comedies and with plays about English history.

The dates of Shakespeare's plays are notoriously hard to determine. Few performances of them were documented; some were not printed until decades after they first appeared on the stage. Mainstream scholars generally place most of the comedies and histories in the 1590s, admitting that this time frame is no more than a widely accepted estimate.

The three parts of *King Henry VI*, culminating in a fourth part, *Richard III*, deal with the long and complex dynastic struggle or civil wars known as the Wars of the Roses (1455–1487), one of England's most turbulent periods. Today it is not easy to follow the plots of these plays.

It may seem strange to us that a young playwright should have written such demanding works early in his career, but they were evidently very popular with the Elizabethan public. Of the four, only *Richard III*, with its wonderfully villainous starring role, is still often performed.

Even today, one of Shakespeare's early comedies, *The Taming of the Shrew*, remains a crowd-pleaser. (It has enjoyed success in a 1999 film adaptation, *10 Things I Hate About You,* with Heath Ledger and Julia Stiles.)

THE "REAL" SHAKESPEARE

AROUND 1850 DOUBTS STARTED TO SURFACE ABOUT WHO HAD ACTUALLY WRITTEN SHAKESPEARE'S PLAYS, CHIEFLY BECAUSE MANY OTHER AUTHORS, SUCH AS MARK TWAIN, THOUGHT THE PLAYS' AUTHOR WAS TOO WELL EDUCATED AND KNOWLEDGEABLE TO HAVE BEEN THE MODESTLY SCHOOLED MAN FROM STRATFORD.

Who, then, was the real author? Many answers have been given, but the three leading candidates are Francis Bacon, Christopher Marlowe, and Edward de Vere, Earl of Oxford.

Francis Bacon (1561-1626)

Bacon was a distinguished lawyer, scientist, philosopher, and essayist. Many considered him one of the great geniuses of his time, capable of any literary achievement, though he wrote little poetry and, as far as we know, no dramas. When people began to suspect that "Shakespeare" was only a pen name, he seemed like a natural candidate. But his writing style was vastly different from the style of the plays.

Christopher Marlowe (1564–1593)

Marlowe wrote several excellent tragedies in a style much like that of the Shakespeare tragedies, though without the comic blend. But he was reportedly killed in a mysterious incident in 1593, before most of the Bard's plays existed. Could his death have been faked? Is it possible that he lived on for decades in hiding, writing under a pen name? This is what his advocates contend.

Edward de Vere, Earl of Oxford (1550–1604)

Oxford is now the most popular and plausible alternative to the lad from Stratford. He had a high reputation as a poet and playwright in his day, but his life was full of scandal. That controversial life seems to match what the poet says about himself in the sonnets, as well as many events in the plays (especially *Hamlet*). However, he died in 1604, and most scholars believe this rules him out as the author of plays that were published after that date.

THE GREAT MAJORITY OF EXPERTS REJECT THESE AND ALL OTHER ALTERNATIVE CANDIDATES, STICKING WITH THE TRADITIONAL VIEW, AFFIRMED IN THE 1623 FIRST FOLIO OF THE PLAYS, THAT THE AUTHOR WAS THE MAN FROM STRATFORD. THAT REMAINS THE SAFEST POSITION TO TAKE, UNLESS STARTLING NEW EVIDENCE TURNS UP, WHICH, AT THIS LATE DATE, SEEMS HIGHLY UNLIKELY.

The story is simple: The enterprising Petruchio resolves to marry a rich young woman, Katherina Minola, for her wealth, despite her reputation for having a bad temper. Nothing she does can discourage this dauntless suitor, and the play ends with Kate becoming a submissive wife. It is all the funnier for being unbelievable.

With *Romeo and Juliet* the Bard created his first enduring triumph. This tragedy of "star-crossed lovers" from feuding families is known around the world. Even people with only the vaguest knowledge of Shakespeare are often aware of this universally beloved story. It has inspired countless similar stories and adaptations, such as the hit musical *West Side Story*.

By the mid-1590s Shakespeare was successful and prosperous, a partner in the Lord Chamberlain's Men. He was rich enough to buy New Place, one of the largest houses in his hometown of Stratford.

Yet, at the peak of his good fortune, came the worst sorrow of his life: Hamnet, his only son, died in August 1596 at the age of eleven, leaving nobody to carry on his family name, which was to die out with his two daughters.

Our only evidence of his son's death is a single line in the parish burial register. As far as we know, this crushing loss left no mark on Shakespeare's work. As far as his creative life shows, it was as if nothing had happened. His silence about his grief may be the greatest puzzle of his mysterious life, although, as we shall see, others remain.

During this period, according to traditional dating (even if it must be somewhat hypothetical), came the torrent of Shakespeare's mightiest works. Among these was another quartet of English history plays, this one centering on the legendary King Henry IV, including *Richard II* and the two parts of *Henry IV*.

Then came a series of wonderful romantic comedies: *Much Ado About Nothing*, *As You Like It*, and *Twelfth Night*.

ACTOR JOSEPH FIENNES PORTRAYED
THE BARD IN THE 1998 FILM
SHAKESPEARE IN LOVE. DIRECTED BY
JOHN MADDEN.

In 1598 the clergyman Francis Meres, as part of a larger work, hailed Shakespeare as the English Ovid, supreme in love poetry as well as drama. "The Muses would speak with Shakespeare's fine filed phrase," Meres wrote, "if they would speak English." He added praise of Shakespeare's "sugared sonnets among his private friends." It is tantalizing; Meres seems to know something of the poet's personal life, but he gives us no hard information. No wonder biographers are frustrated.

Next the Bard returned gloriously to tragedy with *Julius Caesar*. In the play Caesar has returned to Rome in great popularity after his military triumphs.

Brutus and several other leading senators, suspecting that Caesar means to make himself king, plot to assassinate him. Midway through the play, after the assassination, comes one of Shakespeare's most famous scenes. Brutus speaks at Caesar's funeral. But then Caesar's friend Mark Antony delivers a powerful attack on the conspirators, inciting the mob to fury. Brutus and the others, forced to flee Rome, die in the ensuing civil war. In the end the spirit of Caesar wins after all. If Shakespeare had written nothing after *Julius Caesar*, he would still have been remembered as one of the greatest playwrights of all time. But his supreme works were still to come.

Only Shakespeare could have surpassed *Julius Caesar*, and he did so with *Hamlet* (usually dated about 1600). King Hamlet of Denmark has died, apparently bitten by a poisonous snake. Claudius, his brother, has married the dead king's widow, Gertrude, and become the new king, to the disgust and horror of Prince Hamlet. The ghost of old Hamlet appears to young Hamlet, reveals that he was actually poisoned by Claudius, and demands revenge. Hamlet accepts this as his duty, but cannot bring himself to kill his hated uncle. What follows is Shakespeare's most brilliant and controversial plot.

The story of *Hamlet* is set against the religious controversies of the Bard's time. Is the ghost in hell or purgatory? Is Hamlet Catholic or Protestant? Can revenge ever be justified? We are never really given the answers to such questions. But the play reverberates with them.

THE KING'S MEN

In 1603 Queen Elizabeth I died, and King James VI of Scotland became King James I of England. He also became the patron of Shakespeare's acting company, so the Lord Chamberlain's Men became the King's Men. From this point on, we know less of Shakespeare's life in London than in Stratford, where he kept acquiring property.

In the later years of the sixteenth century Shakespeare had been a rather elusive figure in London, delinquent in paying taxes. From 1602 to 1604 he lived, according to his own later testimony, with a French immigrant family named Mountjoy. After 1604 there is no record of any London residence for Shakespeare, nor do we have any reliable recollection of him or his whereabouts by others. As always, the documents leave much to be desired.

Nearly as great as *Hamlet* is *Othello*, and many regard *King Lear*, the heartbreaking tragedy about an old king and his three daughters, as Shakespeare's supreme tragedy. Shakespeare's shortest tragedy, *Macbeth*, tells the story of a Scottish lord and his wife who plot to murder the king of Scotland to gain the throne for themselves. *Antony and Cleopatra*, a sequel to *Julius Caesar*, depicts the aging Mark Antony in love with the enchanting queen of Egypt. *Coriolanus*, another Roman tragedy, is the poet's least popular masterpiece.

SONNETS AND THE END

The year 1609 saw the publication of Shakespeare's Sonnets. Of these 154 puzzling love poems, the first 126 are addressed to a handsome young man, unnamed, but widely believed to be the Earl of Southampton; the rest concern a dark woman, also unidentified. These mysteries are still debated by scholars.

Near the end of his career Shakespeare turned to comedy again, but it was a comedy of a new and more serious kind. Magic plays a large role in these late plays. For example, in *The Tempest*, the exiled duke of Milan, Prospero, uses magic to defeat his enemies and bring about a final reconciliation.

According to the most commonly accepted view, Shakespeare, not yet fifty, retired to Stratford around 1610. He died prosperous in 1616, and left a will that divided his goods, with a famous provision leaving his wife "my second-best bed." He was buried in the chancel of the parish church, under a tombstone bearing a crude rhyme:

> GOOD FRIEND, FOR JESUS SAKE FORBEARE
> TO DIG THE DUST ENCLOSED HERE.
> BLEST BE THE MAN THAT SPARES THESE STONES,
> AND CURSED BE HE THAT MOVES MY BONES.

This epitaph is another hotly debated mystery: Did the great poet actually compose these lines himself?

SHAKESPEARE'S GRAVE IN HOLY TRINITY CHURCH, STRATFORD-UPON-AVON. HIS WIFE, ANNE HATHAWAY, IS BURIED BESIDE HIM.

In 1623 Shakespeare's colleagues of the King's Men produced a large volume of the plays (excluding the sonnets and other poems) titled *The Comedies, Histories, and Tragedies of Mr. William Shakespeare* with a woodcut portrait—the only known portrait—of the Bard. As a literary monument it is priceless, containing our only texts of half the plays; as a source of biographical information it is severely disappointing, giving not even the dates of Shakespeare's birth and death.

Ben Jonson, then England's poet laureate, supplied a long prefatory poem saluting Shakespeare as the equal of the great classical Greek tragedians Aeschylus, Sophocles, and Euripides, adding that "He was not of an age, but for all time."

Some would later denigrate Shakespeare. His reputation took more than a century to conquer Europe, where many regarded him as semi-barbarous. His works were not translated before 1740. Jonson himself, despite his personal affection, would deprecate "idolatry" of the Bard. For a time Jonson himself was considered more "correct" than Shakespeare, and possibly the superior artist.

But Jonson's generous verdict is now the whole world's. Shakespeare was not merely of his own age, "but for all time."

YOU AND I ARE PAST OUR DANCING DAYS

A GLOSSARY OF LITERARY TERMS

allegory—a story in which characters and events stand for general moral truths. Shakespeare never uses this form simply, but his plays are full of allegorical elements.

alliteration—repetition of one or more initial sounds, especially consonants, as in the saying "through thick and thin," or in Julius Caesar's statement, "veni, vidi, vici."

allusion—a reference, especially when the subject referred to is not actually named, but is unmistakably hinted at.

aside—a short speech in which a character speaks to the audience, unheard by other characters on the stage.

comedy—a story written to amuse, using devices such as witty dialogue (high comedy) or silly physical movement (low comedy). Most of Shakespeare's comedies were romantic comedies, incorporating lovers who endure separations, misunderstandings, and other obstacles but who are finally united in a happy resolution.

deus ex machine—an unexpected, artificial resolution to a play's convoluted plot. Literally, "god out of a machine."

dialogue—speech that takes place among two or more characters.

diction—choice of words for tone. A speech's diction may be dignified (as when a king formally addresses his court), comic (as when the ignorant gravediggers debate whether Ophelia deserves a religious funeral), vulgar, romantic, or whatever the dramatic occasion requires. Shakespeare was a master of diction.

Elizabethan—having to do with the reign of Queen Elizabeth I, from 1558 until her death in 1603. This is considered the most famous period in the history of England, chiefly because of Shakespeare and other noted authors (among them Sir Philip Sidney, Edmund Spenser, and Christopher Marlowe). It was also an era of military glory, especially the defeat of the huge Spanish Armada in 1588.

Globe—the Globe Theater housed Shakespeare's acting company, the Lord Chamberlain's Men (later known as the King's Men). Built in 1598, it caught fire and burned down during a performance of *Henry VIII* in 1613.

hyperbole—an excessively elaborate exaggeration used to create special emphasis or a comic effect, as in Montague's remark that his son Romeo's sighs are "adding to clouds more clouds" in *Romeo and Juliet*.

irony—a discrepancy between what a character says and what he or she truly believes, what is expected to happen and what really happens, or between what a character says and what others understand.

metaphor—a figure of speech in which one thing is identified with another, such as when Hamlet calls his father a "fair mountain." (See also **simile**.)

monologue—a speech delivered by a single character.

motif—a recurrent theme or image, such as disease in *Hamlet* or moonlight in *A Midsummer Night's Dream*.

oxymoron—a phrase that combines two contradictory terms, as in the phrase "sounds of silence" or Hamlet's remark, "I must be cruel only to be kind."

personification—imparting personality to something impersonal ("the sky wept"); giving human qualities to an idea or an inanimate object, as in the saying "love is blind."

pun—a playful treatment of words that sound alike, or are exactly the same, but have different meanings. In *Romeo and Juliet* Mercutio says, after being fatally wounded, "Ask for me tomorrow and you shall find me a grave man." "Grave" could mean either a place of burial or serious.

simile—a figure of speech in which one thing is compared to another, usually using the word *like* or *as*. (See also **metaphor**.)

soliloquy—a speech delivered by a single character, addressed to the audience. The most famous are those of Hamlet, but Shakespeare uses this device frequently to tell us his characters' inner thoughts.

symbol—a visible thing that stands for an invisible quality, as poison in *Hamlet* stands for evil and treachery.

syntax—sentence structure or grammar. Shakespeare displays amazing variety of syntax, from the sweet simplicity of his songs to the clotted fury of his great tragic heroes, who can be very difficult to understand at a first hearing. These effects are deliberate; if we are confused, it is because Shakespeare means to confuse us.

theme—the abstract subject or message of a work of art, such as revenge in *Hamlet* or overweening ambition in *Macbeth*.

tone—the style or approach of a work of art. The tone of *A Midsummer Night's Dream*, set by the lovers, Bottom's crew, and the fairies, is light and sweet. The tone of *Macbeth*, set by the witches, is dark and sinister.

tragedy—a story that traces a character's fall from power, sanity, or privilege. Shakespeare's well-known tragedies include *Hamlet, Macbeth,* and *Othello.*

tragicomedy—a story that combines elements of both tragedy and comedy, moving a heavy plot through twists and turns to a happy ending.

verisimilitude—having the appearance of being real or true.

understatement—a statement expressing less than intended, often with an ironic or comic intention; the opposite of hyperbole.

SHAKESPEARE AND
ROMEO AND JULIET

A lobby card for the 1954 ▶
film starring Laurence
Harvey and Susan Shentall

The J. Arthur Rank Organisation presents

Romeo and Juliet

Colour by TECHNICOLOR

LAURENCE
HARVEY

SUSAN
SHENTALL

FLORA
ROBSON

NORMAN
WOOLAND

MERVYN
JOHNS

66929

Chapter One

66929

CHAPTER ONE

Shakespeare and Romeo and Juliet

ROMEO AND JULIET IS ONE OF SHAKESPEARE'S EARLY PLAYS. IT WAS PROBABLY FIRST PERFORMED IN 1594 OR 1595 WHEN LONDON PLAYHOUSES REOPENED AFTER A LONG OUTBREAK OF THE PLAGUE. SOME TEN THOUSAND PEOPLE DIED OF THE DISEASE IN LONDON ALONE. SHAKESPEARE MAKES REFERENCE TO IT IN THE PLAY WHEN A MESSAGE IS NOT DELIVERED BECAUSE OF THE PLAGUE. AT THE FIRST PERFORMANCE, ROMEO WAS PLAYED BY LEADING ACTOR RICHARD BURBAGE, AND JULIET BY MASTER ROBERT GOFFE. WOMEN DID NOT APPEAR LEGALLY ON THE STAGE UNTIL THE LATE SEVENTEENTH CENTURY; UNTIL THEN FEMALE PARTS WERE PLAYED BY YOUNG BOYS.

Like all great playwrights or novelists, William Shakespeare wrote about things he knew. The influence of the society in which he lived is obvious in his works. A major example is the role of Juliet. The queen may have been God's deputy in Elizabethan England, but female power largely began and ended with her. There was a great difference in lifestyle between men and women of the time. As a young woman, Juliet had no power or even a choice in social situations. Her life was under the control of men, first her father and then, presumably, the man her father chose to be her husband. In this case she defied convention by secretly marrying Romeo. However, the fact that her father could—and did—arrange for her marriage to Paris shows the power that men held over women at the time. It also sealed Juliet's fate.

Social structure was tight and fixed in Elizabethan society, as evidenced in *Romeo and Juliet*. Because she is a woman, Juliet has no power. Because Peter, servant to the Capulets, is poorly educated and cannot read, he has no power either. His illiteracy and his status bind him forever within the social structure. That rigid structure weaves into the events that unfold as Shakespeare tells his story of tragic love.

Romeo and Juliet is often called the most famous example of young love, the tragedy of love, or the ultimate love story. But it is actually as much about hate as it is about love. Besides the story of a tragic marriage, it tells of two families and the deadly feud that rules their lives and those of the people who surround them.

Shakespeare did not make up the story of Romeo and Juliet. Nor did he introduce the theme to theater audiences. It was already a popular

THESE VIOLENT DELIGHTS HAVE VIOLENT ENDS

tale in European folklore when it was translated in 1562 into English in a poem by Arthur Brooke called *The Tragicall Historye of Romeus and Juliet*. Shakespeare embellished the old story and adapted it for the stage. He contrasted the innocence of the young lovers with the almost crude sexuality of other characters. He shortened the time frame in Brooke's poem from months to just four days. That allowed just a single night for the lovers to spend together. Shakespeare lengthened Mercutio's role with a speech about fairy queen Mab. In Brooke's poem, Romeo kills Tybalt in self-defense. However, Shakespeare has Tybalt kill Mercutio, which drives Romeo to fight and kill him. Shakespeare also changed Juliet's age from sixteen to thirteen to make her appear more vulnerable. He makes her father move the wedding day ahead from Thursday to Wednesday. These and other changes emphasize speed, and how quickly the young couple becomes involved in love and passion. This sense of urgency creates the intense pressure that inevitably leads to tragedy and death.

Each of the prologues to Acts I and II, as well as the first conversation between Romeo and Juliet in Act I, Scene 5, contains a sonnet, a fourteen-line lyric poem with a formal rhyme pattern.

Sonnets often spoke of troubled love, so Shakespeare opens his play with a sonnet to establish the themes of love and hate, or conflict, that will emerge. And these first lines of the Act I prologue establish the entire conflict and action of the play. They tell of the bitter feud between the two noble families of Verona. They speak of the star-crossed lovers who will lose their lives because of the feud.

When the lovers first meet in Act I, Scene 5, Shakespeare again uses the sonnet to underscore the depth of Romeo's initial attraction to Juliet:

O, SHE DOTH TEACH THE TORCHES TO BURN BRIGHT!
IT SEEMS SHE HANGS UPON THE CHEEK OF NIGHT. . . .

He compares the light of Juliet's inner and outer beauty to that of a brilliant star. Once again Shakespeare uses the image of star-crossed lovers to warn the audience of their inevitable fate.

Though the story of *Romeo and Juliet* was not new, Shakespeare's skill in making subtle changes brought out the individuality of his characters, distinguishing him from most other artists of his time and since. He took a theme that was already known to theatergoers and created what is usually regarded as the greatest love story of all time.

AN
EXCELLENT
conceited Tragedie
OF
Romeo and Iuliet.

As it hath been often (with great applause) plaid publiquely, by the right Honourable the L. of *Hunfdon* his Seruants.

LONDON,
Printed by Iohn Danter.
1597.

THE FIRST PRINTED TEXT, Q1 OR THE "BAD QUARTO," WAS HASTILY PUT TOGETHER, CUT BY SOME 800 LINES.

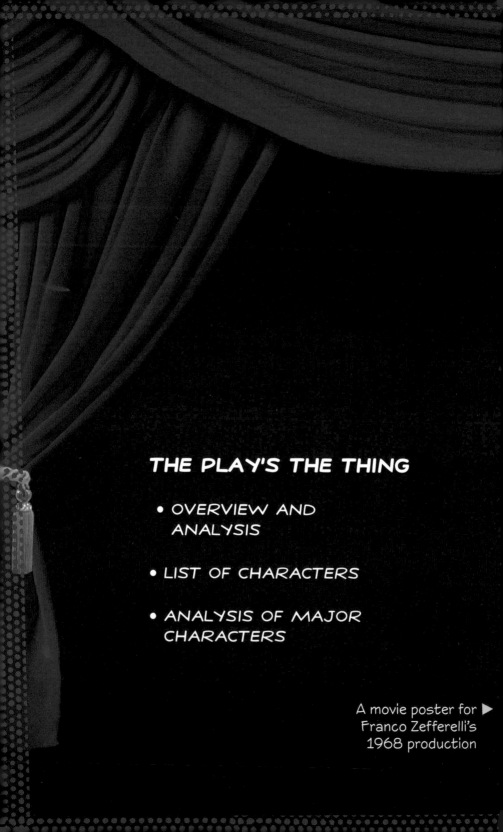

THE PLAY'S THE THING

- OVERVIEW AND ANALYSIS

- LIST OF CHARACTERS

- ANALYSIS OF MAJOR CHARACTERS

A movie poster for ▶
Franco Zefferelli's
1968 production

ROMEO & JULIET

Chapter Two

66929   66929

CHAPTER
TWO

The Play's the Thing

ACT I, PROLOGUE

OVERVIEW

The Chorus (presented as only one character) enters and describes the noble households of Capulet and Montague in a sonnet:

> TWO HOUSEHOLDS, BOTH ALIKE IN DIGNITY,
> IN FAIR VERONA, WHERE WE LAY OUR SCENE,

The ancient grudge between them has become a violent and bloody conflict:

> FROM ANCIENT GRUDGE BREAK TO NEW MUTINY,
> WHERE CIVIL BLOOD MAKES CIVIL HANDS UNCLEAN.

Romeo and Juliet are described as victims of fate:

> FROM FORTH THE FATAL LOINS OF THESE TWO FOES
> A PAIR OF STAR-CROSSED LOVERS TAKE THEIR LIFE;

And there is no mistaking the outcome of this tragedy:

> WHOLE MISADVENTURED PITEOUS OVERTHROWS
> DO WITH THEIR DEATH BURY THEIR PARENTS' STRIFE

ANALYSIS

The Chorus not only sets the scene, providing background information, but also tells the audience exactly what will happen. The phrase *star-crossed* is used because, at that time, stars were thought to control human destiny. The lack of suspense about the outcome emphasizes a major theme in the tragedy. It is fate. From the very beginning of the play, the audience realizes that the young lovers will die. Death is their fate. There is no escape.

ACT 1, SCENE 1

OVERVIEW

Two Capulet house servants, Sampson and Gregory, spend time in loud, boastful, and vulgar conversation, most of which concerns the character of Montague men and women and what members of the Capulet household will do to them. When servants of the Montague household enter, they are immediately drawn into a Verona street brawl. One of the Montagues, Benvolio, Romeo's cousin, comes upon this conflict. A peacemaker (his name means "goodwill"), Benvolio draws his sword in an attempt to stop the fighting. At that moment, the fiery Capulet kinsman Tybalt enters. When he sees Benvolio's drawn sword, he needs no other excuse to attack. Now the brawl widens, as many citizens become involved.

At this point, the heads of the two feuding households, Montague and Capulet, arrive with their wives. Instead of calming the scene, they want to attack one another, but their wives intervene. Prince Escalus, who is in charge of law and order in Verona, enters and orders everyone to throw down their weapons and stop the fighting. He declares that the feud between the two families has gone on far too long and must stop. He pronounces a death sentence for anyone who further disturbs the peace.

Everyone now disperses except for Montague, Lady Montague, and their nephew Benvolio. The Montagues speak of their worry over their son Romeo, who seems to be melancholy lately. Benvolio promises to find out what is troubling the young man. The parents leave, and a saddened young Romeo enters. He tells Benvolio that he is in love with a beautiful young woman named Rosaline, but that she spurns him. Benvolio says that Romeo must forget Rosaline, but Romeo says he cannot.

ANALYSIS

The rousing action of the opening street brawl introduces all of the layers of Verona's society that are important to the play. It also stresses an important concept in Elizabethan England and this play: masculine honor. No matter the consequences, a man of Verona—whether he is a servant or noble—must defend his honor against any transgression. How easily this concept leads to trouble is seen in the characters of peacemaker Benvolio and hot-tempered Tybalt. Benvolio draws his sword with the idea that it will make the troublemakers back away. Tybalt immediately sees a drawn sword as an invitation to a duel.

Romeo, the protagonist and lover, enters at the end of the scene. It is here that the focus switches from hate to love. Expecting talk of Romeo's love for Juliet, the audience is shocked to find out that he is in love with Rosaline. At this early point in the play, Romeo is shown as a young man more in love with the idea of love than with an actual person. He even speaks in a youthful manner, which changes to more mature verse as he falls in love with Juliet. Romeo also speaks of love in military terms, stressing Shakespeare's idea of how close love and hate can be.

ACT I, SCENE 2

OVERVIEW

Capulet walks on a street in Verona engaged in conversation with Count Paris, who speaks of his wish to marry Juliet. Capulet is pleased, for he knows that Paris is a noble kinsman of Prince Escalus. Yet, as a father who professes love for his thirteen-year-old daughter, Capulet tells Paris that Juliet is too young to marry. The marriage must be postponed for two years. However, to indicate that he is in favor of the union, Capulet invites Paris to a masquerade that evening. In that way, Paris can begin to know Juliet and even win affection from her.

Capulet calls his servant Peter, giving him a list of people to invite to the feast. The two men leave and Peter is left alone. He worries about how to do as his master asks because he cannot read the names on the list. When Romeo and Benvolio stroll by, Peter asks Romeo to read the list to him. Romeo sees that Rosaline is on the list. Peter just assumes that Romeo and Benvolio are not Montagues, who would, of course, not be welcome, so he invites them to the masquerade. Romeo agrees, thinking he will see Rosaline there. Benvolio goes along with this idea, believing that the sight of other beautiful women will distract Romeo from his infatuation with Rosaline.

ANALYSIS

Count Paris is introduced as Capulet's choice of a husband for Juliet. In addition, the audience learns that Romeo and Juliet are going to meet, and the expectations are that the young man's feelings about Rosaline are going to change. Through the conversation between Paris and Capulet, Juliet's social status is clearly established. As a young woman of Verona, she has no power and no say in any situation that concerns her future. Although Capulet appears to want what is best for his daughter, Paris's position as a relative of the prince is obviously of greater importance than Juliet's happiness. Capulet speaks of his daughter's youth and innocence. That may indicate parental concern; it may also be thrown out as an enticement for Paris. And although Capulet insists that the marriage must wait two years, he immediately invites Paris to the feast so that he might begin to court the young girl.

The audience realizes even at this early stage that circumstances have already sealed Romeo and Juliet's fate before they meet. The two unknowing rivals are contrasted: Paris, the courteous, well-to-do suitor, and Romeo, the idealistic youth who is in love with love. The servant Peter provides humor but indicates that the poor and illiterate also have no power in Veronese society.

ACT I, SCENE 3

OVERVIEW

Prior to the masquerade, Lady Capulet asks the Nurse to find her daughter. Nurse is Juliet's nanny and helped to raise her. Once Juliet arrives, Lady Capulet sends the Nurse away, but quickly changes her mind and asks her to stay to give whatever counsel she can in the conversation. However, the Nurse begins a long story that links Juliet as an innocent bystander to a sexual joke some years earlier. In effect, an incident where she fell on her back as a toddler inspired a lewd comment made by Nurse's husband that Juliet will do so again with a sexual partner when she is grown. Juliet is embarrassed, but Lady Capulet cannot get the Nurse to stop her story.

Finally, when the Nurse mentions marriage, Lady Capulet says that is what she wished to discuss with her daughter. She asks Juliet if she has given any thought to marriage. Juliet says it is an honor that she has not considered. When her mother says that Paris is interested in her, Juliet dutifully replies that she will talk to him at the feast.

ANALYSIS

This is our first look at the other title character. Once again, Juliet's lack of power over her own life is introduced. Her mother, who was herself married at a young age, agrees with her husband that Paris is a good prospective husband for Juliet. The Nurse is shown as a comic character; her coarse outlook on life is contrasted with Juliet's innocence. Her tale of the joke indicates that, since birth, Juliet has been viewed as a potential sexual partner for her husband in marriage.

The relationship between mother and daughter is clear in this scene. Lady Capulet is shown as cold and distant. She wants only for Juliet to obey her father's wishes, with which she concurs. She, too, sees the union with Paris as a social boon for the family and makes no attempt to consider her daughter's feelings in the matter. Since she regards marriage as a way to increase wealth, and because the Nurse regards marriage as nothing more than a sexual act, neither woman can understand a romantic concept of love.

Juliet is clearly not in favor of an arranged marriage when her mother asks if she would be agreeable to marrying Paris. The young girl cleverly replies that she will meet him and see what she thinks: "I'll look to like, if looking liking move / But no more deep will I endart my eye. . . ." Young and innocent as she is, Juliet's answer indicates her growing emotional maturity. She has no intention of marrying someone she does not love. Although Juliet's innocence is stressed, an inner strength appears. Her evasive answer to her mother will blossom into her defiance against her parents later in the play.

OVERVIEW

Wearing masks, Romeo, Benvolio, and their friend Mercutio join other masked guests on their way to the feast at the Capulets' house. Romeo worries that, as Montagues, they will not be allowed to enter. His friends laugh at that concern. The still-melancholy Romeo says that, even if they are allowed in, he will not dance. Mercutio begins to mock him and turns all of Romeo's statements of love into sexual references. Finally Mercutio

ROMEO AND HIS FRIENDS
PREPARE TO ENTER THE CAPULET FEAST
IN THE ROYAL SHAKESPEARE COMPANY'S 1976
PRODUCTION, DIRECTED BY TREVOR NUNN

launches into the tale of Queen Mab of the fairies and becomes quite passionate in his delivery. Romeo steps in and calms him down. As the three continue to the hall, Romeo voices concern about the night's activities, fearing that they might eventually lead to death. However, with his friends around him, he shrugs off his fears and continues to the feast.

ANALYSIS

The clever and witty Mercutio is introduced in this scene. His Queen Mab speech is one of the play's most famous. He talks of the fairy queen who gives people dreams as she rides through the night on her tiny wagon. But the dreams she brings usually are not good for the sleepers. Instead the dreams only fortify whatever vice the sleeper has, such as lust or violence. In his highly nonsensical but colorful speech, Mercutio suggests that fantasies and desires like the ones Romeo exhibits are silly and fragile, as is the fairy queen. Such a suggestion is in sharp contrast to both Romeo and Juliet, who view true love as a noble condition. Here Mercutio proves himself to be a master of puns. He is also shown as the friend who can jest with Romeo as no one else can. He is as down-to-earth as Romeo is a daydreamer. His energetic character is established, not only as a foil to Romeo's seriousness, but also so that the audience will have sympathy for him when he is accidentally killed in Act III.

This scene does not move the plot forward, since the audience already knows that Romeo and his friends are going to the feast. The audience also already knows that Romeo will suffer an untimely death, but his references to death point to the general sense of fate taking over the characters. In fact, his final speech in the scene indicates impending doom, which casts a shadow on the feast itself. Once again, the image of star-crossed lovers emerges. Their destinies will lead to tragedy.

In this scene, for the first time, the audience becomes aware of a tragic tone. *Romeo and Juliet* is often spoken of as a great tragedy. What is tragedy? It is usually defined as a story or play that deals with a serious theme and ends with someone's downfall or destruction. But when one first reads *Romeo and Juliet,* it does not seem like a tragedy. Although the play opens with a street brawl, the brawlers are almost comic characters who are fighting over trivia. It all ends peaceably when the prince scolds them and sends them home. The rest of the scene concerns Romeo's melancholy over the indifferent Rosaline. This may be sad for Romeo, but it is still not a tragedy. But in Scene 4, the audience senses that tragedy will follow. Something is afoot; there is trouble ahead. The scene is made even more somber by the knowledge that Tybalt will seek out Romeo for revenge.

ACT I, SCENE 5

OVERVIEW

The scene opens in the great hall of the Capulets, with the masked ball in full swing. Capulet interacts with his guests, particularly his nephew Tybalt. Romeo enters and sees Juliet across the room. He asks a servant to identify her, but the servant replies that he does not know her name. From that moment on, Rosaline no longer exists, and Romeo knows that he has never been in love until this moment. As he speaks aloud of his feelings, Tybalt, who is wandering through the crowd, recognizes Romeo's voice. Tybalt knows that Romeo is a Montague and calls for a servant to bring him his sword. He intends to fight the intruder who has crashed the party. But Capulet intervenes, saying that Romeo has a good reputation in Verona, and Capulet will not have any bloodshed at his feast. He makes Tybalt agree not to cause any problems. Although he feels his honor has been slighted, Tybalt obeys his uncle and secretly vows to get revenge on Romeo.

Romeo crosses the room and boldly approaches Juliet. In the form of the first four lines of a sonnet, he speaks of himself as a pilgrim who needs her saintly kiss to absolve him of sin. Juliet responds by continuing the

LAUREN AMBROSE AND OSCAR ISAAC
PLAYED THE LOVERS AT THE DELACORTE
THEATER IN NEW YORK CITY'S
CENTRAL PARK, 2007.

sonnet, then quietly allows the kiss. Then she asks if her lips now contain his sin since they have kissed: "Then have my lips the sin that they have took." Romeo wants his sin back, so they kiss again. At this point, the Nurse appears and tells Juliet that her mother wants her. Romeo asks the Nurse who Juliet is and is devastated to learn that Juliet's mother is Lady Capulet. Benvolio arrives to take Romeo home from the feast.

Now Juliet asks the Nurse to learn the identity of this mysterious man with whom she has fallen instantly in love. She fears she will die if she finds out that he is married. Instead she is appalled to discover that she has fallen in love with a Montague. Following the Nurse, she leaves the hall.

ANALYSIS

The first meeting of the lovers, anticipated by the audience, takes over the scene. Delaying their first meeting until the end of Act I is well justified by the poetic language, which casts a spell of wonder and excitement. Struck by her beauty, Romeo engages Juliet in a conversation that is tinged with religion. It indicates that their love will become associated with divine purity and passion. Before their first kiss, Romeo and Juliet speak the fourteen lines of a sonnet, which Shakespeare uses to express their perfect love. Romeo indicates that he can now tell the difference between his anguish over Rosaline and what he is experiencing at this moment: "I ne'er saw true beauty till this night." He is changing before the audience's eyes from a young boy in love with love to a man who has caught the beginnings of true passion.

In the first kiss Romeo is the initiator, but Juliet uses language that encourages the second kiss. With that short exchange, the innocent young girl becomes one who understands what she is suddenly feeling and what she wants. This sense of immediate rapture between the two is emphasized by the fact that neither Romeo nor Juliet thinks to ask the other's name.

In spite of the initial wonder of their love, the scene carries a mood of impending tragedy, which the audience immediately recognizes. The hot-headed Tybalt endures what he feels is an insult. The audience realizes that there will be trouble between him and Romeo. Tybalt will at some point ignore his uncle's wish to leave Romeo alone. This shows that the feud between the two families extends not just to heads of the households but throughout the families and across generations.

Even before Juliet learns Romeo's identity, she says she would die if she would not be able to marry him. The image that identifies death as Juliet's bridegroom occurs often during the play. This first meeting between the star-crossed lovers sends them on the first step toward their deaths.

ACT II, PROLOGUE

OVERVIEW

The Chorus enters with another sonnet, which expresses how both Romeo and Juliet feel after meeting:

> NOW ROMEO IS BELOVED AND LOVES AGAIN,
> ALIKE BEWITCHED BY THE CHARM OF LOOKS

and the troubles they will suffer because of their two families:

> BEING HELD A FOE, HE MAY NOT HAVE ACCESS
> TO BREATHE SUCH VOWS AS LOVERS USE TO SWEAR.

ANALYSIS

The Prologue helps build suspense by stressing the problems that the lovers face. It also contrasts Romeo's rejected love for Rosaline and the mutual passion that is immediately evident with Juliet. Because it does little to move the story along, the Prologue is sometimes omitted when the play is performed. Some critics have suggested that the Prologue was added sometime after the play was written. However, it does help indicate that the lovers will be together despite the problems that confront them.

ACT II, SCENE 1

OVERVIEW

After leaving the feast, Romeo decides he must find Juliet. He enters the

Capulet property and leaps over a wall into the orchard. Mercutio and Benvolio enter the lane near the garden and call out to him. They are sure he is nearby, but Romeo does not answer. Amused and somewhat annoyed, Mercutio launches into a rather obscene and mocking speech about Romeo and his former love, Rosaline. Romeo hears the speech but does not want to be found, so he does not respond. Then Mercutio and Benvolio leave.

ANALYSIS

This scene contrasts Mercutio's understanding of love as a physical conquest and the sense that Romeo has moved beyond that in his feeling for Juliet. His leap over the wall signifies this change. He has moved beyond his friend. In addition, Romeo's leap over the wall signifies that he is separating from friends and family in order to be with Juliet.

Scenes like this one mainly take place very early in the morning or very late at night. Shakespeare has to use the hours of a full day to keep the action compressed into a four-day sequence.

ACT II, SCENE 2

OVERVIEW

With Romeo silent in the orchard, Juliet appears at a window in the Capulet house above. He does not speak to her but compares her to the morning sun, far more beautiful than the moon it takes away. Not aware of his presence, Juliet speaks aloud about the fate that has placed her and Romeo in two warring families. She bemoans their names, saying that she would refuse her name if he said he loved her, or she would become his if he refused the Montague name. At this point, Romeo answers her, but she is afraid that he will be killed if he is discovered.

The two speak of love, with Juliet growing afraid that they have found this passion too quickly. Romeo reassures her that their love is real. She

JULIET (CLAIRE HOLMAN) BIDS GOOD NIGHT TO ROMEO (MICHAEL MALONEY) DURING THE BALCONY SCENE AT THE BARBICAN THEATER, LONDON, 1992.

disappears and reappears at the window as the Nurse repeatedly calls to her. Finally Juliet appears and tells Romeo that a messenger will seek him out the following day to confirm Romeo's intention to wed her. Juliet goes into her chamber, and Romeo departs.

ANALYSIS

In what is one of the most famous scenes in theater, the joy and romance of young love dominate the action. This is also the happiest and least tragic scene of the play, filled with lovely poetic images. It is usually called "The Balcony Scene," since Juliet often appears standing on a balcony. It is believed, however, that the scene was initially written with Juliet at her window. In his passion, Romeo describes Juliet as the sun, meaning that their love moves him into spiritual light. Yet it is obvious that their circumstances indicate that they must meet in darkness.

Romeo begins to mature in this scene, indicated by the fact that he speaks more in blank verse than in the rhymed verse that he used earlier. Yet Juliet remains the more mature of the two at this point. It is she who mentions marriage, for instance, and makes the arrangements for a meeting the next day. Her reference to the family names points out a major conflict, the feud between the families that will lead to their deaths. Her comings and goings from the window (or balcony) heighten the tension and speed up the action of the play. In addition, Juliet tells Romeo:

> AND ALL MY FORTUNES AT THY FOOT I'LL LAY
> AND FOLLOW THEE, MY LORD, THROUGHOUT THE WORLD.

It is an ironic promise, since she will, indeed, follow him into death.

ACT II, SCENE 3

OVERVIEW

In the early morning hours, Friar Lawrence, a Franciscan friar, has been collecting herbs, weeds, and flowers from his garden. He speaks of the benefits of these plants, showing a good knowledge of their properties. When Romeo enters, the Friar senses that the young man has been out all night and fears that he has slept with Rosaline, which the Friar would consider a sin. Instead he is surprised to learn that Romeo is passionately in love with Juliet and wants to marry her. This shocks the Friar because of its suddenness. He comments that young love is often fickle, but Romeo

WISELY AND SLOW; THEY STUMBLE THAT RUN FAST.

protests. He tells the Friar that his love is true and that Juliet feels the same way. The Friar is not convinced. However, he does agree to marry them. Perhaps this marriage, thinks the well-meaning Friar, will end the brutal and senseless feud between two of the most prominent families of Verona.

ANALYSIS

This introduction of the Friar highlights the tension between good and evil. He wants to end the bitter feud between the two families. That is why he agrees to marry the young lovers. The Friar is also an expert on medicinal plants. He speaks knowingly of both their healing and harming powers. This dual nature of plants suggests that good and evil live together both in nature and in people. The pull between good and evil is constant throughout the play. The Friar himself is a good example of a man with conflicting characteristics. His heart is in the right place; he really wants to bring peace to Verona and he wants to bring happiness to Romeo and Juliet. But his method of doing so is to marry the young couple without their families' knowledge. His well-intentioned plan to help the couple ultimately leads to tragedy for both families.

Friar Lawrence is both a confidant and father figure to Romeo. The relationship between the two highlights the theme of youth versus old age, which is constant throughout the play. Romeo tells no one except the Friar about his feelings for Juliet, a fact that also highlights the young man's growing isolation from his family and friends. As a young man in love, Romeo is eager to get married. He wants the Friar to marry him and Juliet that very day. But the Friar, not convinced of Romeo's true feelings, advises restraint.

ACT II, SCENE 4

OVERVIEW

On a street in Verona, Mercutio wonders aloud where Romeo spent the previous night because he did not return home. Benvolio says that Tybalt has sent a letter to the Montague household. Still suffering an imagined insult because of Romeo's attendance at the Capulet feast, Tybalt has challenged Romeo to a duel. Mercutio laughingly replies that Romeo is already dead because he has been struck by Cupid's arrow. When Romeo arrives, Mercutio continues his teasing about what he still thinks is Romeo's love for Rosaline. The two young men carry on some sexual verbal jousting.

The Nurse and the servant Peter arrive looking for Romeo. Mercutio begins to tease the Nurse about being a harlot. After Mercutio and Benvolio leave, the Nurse warns Romeo that he must not fool with Juliet's feelings. He declares that he will not. He says they will be married that afternoon if the Nurse can get Juliet to the Friar's cell. The Nurse agrees to carry the message and also agrees to receive a rope ladder from a servant of his so that Romeo can spend their wedding night in Juliet's chamber.

ANALYSIS

The sexual banter between Romeo and Mercutio contrasts with the impending disaster that is noted in Tybalt's challenge to a duel. Tybalt is quick-tempered and vengeful. Romeo, once depressed and melancholy,

"MY MAN'S AS TRUE AS STEEL."

is now above this. He thinks only of his all-consuming love for Juliet. His elation is such that he can answer Mercutio's barbed remarks with equally lively retorts. Mercutio's comments are ironic, since he still believes Romeo is passionate about Rosaline.

Mercutio's quick-tempered nature comes forth in this scene. He shows a growing antagonism for Tybalt and scorns Tybalt's challenge. Again, the feeling of urgency is portrayed, as is the contrast between love and hate. Tybalt is always ready for a fight, and he has made it his responsibility to carry on the hostility between the warring families. Romeo, on the other hand, has risen above such concerns in his love for Juliet.

There are many references to time throughout this scene. Time plays a very important role in the tragedy. The period from when the lovers meet at the feast and fall in love until their wedding night covers just twenty-four hours.

ACT II, SCENE 5

OVERVIEW

Juliet has been waiting impatiently in her garden for three hours for the Nurse to return with news of Romeo. Finally the Nurse arrives. She teases that she is too out of breath to tell Juliet the news. But she relents and says that Juliet is to meet Romeo at the Friar's, where they will be married. Meanwhile the Nurse is to await Romeo's servant, who is bringing the ladder so Romeo can enter Juliet's chamber that night.

ANALYSIS

The speed of the events in the preceding scene contrasts with the hours that Juliet waited to hear the news. This scene is all about the wonder and the elation of romantic love. Both lovers are filled with anticipation. Unlike in the previous scenes, Juliet acts much like the thirteen-year-old that she is as she thinks about her feelings for Romeo. This also contrasts

THE NURSE (BETTE BOURNE) AND JULIET (KANANU KIRIMI) SHARE A SCENE IN ACT II OF A PRODUCTION AT THE GLOBE THEATER, 2004.

with the slow movements of the Nurse. She makes Juliet frantic with her deliberate and slow tale before she reveals what Romeo said about the time and place of the marriage. Like Mercutio's, the Nurse's view is that love is no more than a physical relationship, and she also shares his bawdy sense of humor. She touches once again on life and death when she comments that Juliet will have pleasure on her wedding night, with the hint that pregnancy will follow. The audience knows that Juliet will marry but will not live to bear children.

ACT II, SCENE 6

OVERVIEW

Romeo waits in the Friar's cell for Juliet to arrive. He speaks of the joy and passion that he feels, but the Friar cautions him to love more moderately. However, when Juliet arrives, Romeo showers her with romantic words. The Friar realizes that moderation will not work at this moment. He says, "Come, come with me, and we will make short work;/For, by your leaves, you shall not stay alone,/Till Holy Church incorporate two in one." Then the three exit to go to the wedding ceremony.

ANALYSIS

Two things highlight the wedding scene. It is very brief, and for all its atmosphere of love's beauty, there is a feeling of impending doom. The Friar speaks of Romeo and Juliet's passion, warning, "These violent delights have violent ends." He calls for moderation. Yet that is not the way that Romeo and Juliet, or any of the other characters, live their lives. The passion of the young lovers is portrayed as beautiful poetry, but in the end it will prove destructive. Romeo says, "Then love-devouring Death do what he dare—/It is enough I may but call her mine." He is saying that the happiness he feels in marrying Juliet cannot even be marred by the appearance of death. His words, of course, foreshadow the fact that death will indeed be victorious over them both.

ACT III, SCENE 1

OVERVIEW

On the street later that afternoon, Benvolio, not wanting another brawl, tells Mercutio that perhaps they should go indoors because he is afraid they might meet men from the Capulet household. Mercutio scorns that

A PAINTING BY EDWIN A. ABBEY, "THE DEATH OF MERCUTIO," APPEARED IN *HARPER'S MONTHLY MAGAZINE,* JULY, 1903

idea. Not long after, Tybalt and his friends appear. Tybalt asks to speak to them, which annoys Mercutio, who starts to provoke him. When Romeo enters, Tybalt dares him to fight. But Romeo, who is now married to Juliet and therefore is kin to Tybalt, says that he does not wish to fight. He remarks that Tybalt will understand his refusal when he learns the reason for it. At this point Mercutio, who does not understand Romeo's reluctance to fight, becomes even more annoyed. He declares that he will fight Tybalt. Because Tybalt can let no remark go unchallenged, he immediately draws his sword. Romeo tries to get between the two men, but Mercutio is stabbed. Tybalt and his men leave, and Mercutio exits to die, blaming both families by cursing, "A plague o' both your houses."

Romeo is now enraged at himself for being cowardly and causing his friend's death:

> THIS GENTLEMAN, THE PRINCE'S NEAR ALLY
> MY VERY FRIEND, HATH GOT THIS MORTAL HURT
> IN MY BEHALF; MY REPUTATION STAINED
> WITH TYBALT'S SLANDER TYBALT, THAT AN HOUR
> HATH BEEN MY COUSIN! O SWEET JULIET,
> THY BEAUTY HATH MADE ME EFFEMINATE
> AND IN MY TEMPER SOFTENED VALOR'S STEEL!

Tybalt reenters, and Romeo draws his sword. Once again Tybalt responds. In the ensuing battle, Romeo kills Tybalt. Benvolio, who sees a crowd approaching, tells Romeo to flee, which he does.

A crowd of citizens appears, along with Prince Escalus and the Montagues and Capulets. Benvolio explains to the prince that Romeo tried to stop the initial fight between Tybalt and Mercutio. Lady Capulet, however, says that Benvolio is lying: "Affection makes him false, he speaks not true." She demands Romeo's death: "Romeo slew Tybalt; Romeo must not live." Instead the prince orders Romeo to be exiled from Verona. If he does not leave the city, he will be put to death.

ANALYSIS

At this point and from now on, the sudden death of Mercutio assures the audience that the play will be taking a tragic turn. The emphasis upon love in the previous scene now turns dramatically to death and violence. It is obvious that what really matters in Verona is masculine honor. Impulsively Romeo becomes enraged at himself because he let his joy over marrying Juliet turn him into a coward. The result is Mercutio's death. In the society of the time, it was generally believed that a man who was too much in love was unmanly. In fact Romeo speaks of himself as "effeminate."

Ironically Mercutio dies thinking his fatal injury stems from the feud between the two houses. He never finds out about Romeo's love for Juliet. Even more ironic is Romeo's attack on Tybalt, which results from his rage over Mercutio's death. By killing Tybalt in fury, Romeo acts the same way as the quick-tempered Tybalt and Mercutio and the heads of the two households who carry on the feud. Another irony is that Romeo's refusal to fight Tybalt results in the very violence he tried to avoid. At every step throughout the scene, passion overcomes reason.

ACT III, SCENE 2

OVERVIEW

Juliet impatiently waits in the orchard, longing for darkness so that Romeo will join her "untalked of and unseen" for their wedding night. The Nurse appears with excited news of the duel between Romeo and Tybalt. The Nurse's jumble of hasty words leads Juliet to believe that Romeo is dead. The distraught Nurse tries to explain further through her moans. Now Juliet thinks that both Romeo and Tybalt have died. At last the Nurse calms down and is able to explain herself. But when Juliet learns that Romeo has killed Tybalt and has been exiled, she faults him for his rashness. The Nurse quickly agrees, and she, too, criticizes Romeo. Now Juliet chides the Nurse and herself for criticizing Romeo. She moans aloud that there will be no wedding night because Romeo is banished. The Nurse, however, says she knows where Romeo is hiding and assures Juliet that he will come to her. Juliet gives the Nurse a ring to give to Romeo: "Give this ring to my true knight,/And bid him come to take his last farewell."

"COME, LOVING BLACK BROW'D NIGHT"

The ever-present sense of impending doom is again evident in this scene. Juliet impatiently waits in the orchard for night to arrive, expressing her frustration at the slow pace of the daylight hours with her repeated exhortations to "come, night." Meanwhile the audience already knows about the tragedy that has occurred. The differences between the Nurse and Juliet, old age versus youth, are accented here. The Nurse blames Romeo because she views life without emotion. Romeo has killed a Capulet; therefore, Romeo must be punished. "Shame come to Romeo," she says to Juliet. The Nurse cannot understand the depth of Juliet's love. Juliet, who initially felt conflicted between Romeo and her cousin Tybalt, quickly realizes that her loyalty is to her husband. As Romeo is leaving his friends and family behind, so Juliet, too, is leaving the Capulets to share a life with her husband. She is emerging as a young woman with her own opinions and emotions. The split between Juliet and the Nurse widens as Juliet realizes that she can no longer count on the older woman for guidance. This split will grow even wider in Scene 5.

Shakespeare often links young love with suicide and death, and there is great psychological tension in this scene. When Juliet mistakenly believes Romeo is dead, she assumes that he killed himself and that she will do the same. Even when she knows that he is alive but has been banished, she equates banishment with doom. She says that she will go to her wedding bed, not with Romeo, but with death.

Light and dark images are important in creating the mood of this scene and also hint at what is to follow. As Juliet waits in the orchard for news, she views the approaching night with pleasure because Romeo will be with her. It is in darkness that they will share their love, and, as the audience knows, it is in darkness that they will enter eternity.

ACT III, SCENE 3

OVERVIEW

In the Friar's cell, Romeo waits for news of his fate for killing Tybalt. When the Friar enters and tells him that he is fortunate because the sentence is banishment, not death, Romeo is distraught. He says that the sentence is far worse than death because he cannot live without Juliet. In desperation, he ignores the Friar's attempts to comfort him and falls to the floor.

The Nurse enters. Thinking that Juliet now regards him as a murderer for killing her cousin, Romeo threatens to stab himself. The Friar chides him for being unmanly and offers a plan. Romeo will see Juliet that night, but he must leave her and Verona before the morning light. He will stay in Mantua while the Friar spreads the news about their marriage. The Friar hopes such news will end the feud and unite the families. Romeo agrees, joyfully accepts Juliet's ring from the Nurse, and says good-bye to the Friar.

ANALYSIS

The emotional differences between Romeo and Juliet are contrasted here. When Juliet thinks she has to live without Romeo, she is grief-stricken and bemoans her fate. When Romeo thinks he must live without Juliet, he tries to stab himself and end the suffering. Also, at this point in his heightened emotions, Romeo cannot accept the calm reasoning of the Friar. Once again there is the conflict between young and old. The Friar does not comprehend the depth of Romeo's passion, and that very passion prevents Romeo from following the rational advice that might otherwise have changed his fate.

Once again the marriage of the young lovers is linked to death. In the previous scene, Juliet likened Romeo's banishment to a kind of death. When he hears his punishment in this scene, Romeo, too, speaks of death: "Ha, banishment? Be merciful, say 'death';/For exile hath more terror in his look,/Much more than death. Do not say banishment." The Friar himself links the marriage to death: "Affliction is enamored of thy parts/ And thou art wedded to calamity." But no matter how the Friar tries to reason with him, Romeo is too upset with his sentence to accept the older man's assurances.

ACT III, SCENE 4

OVERVIEW

Capulet, Lady Capulet, and Paris meet after the death of Tybalt. Capulet tells Paris that, despite the tragedy, he thinks his daughter will abide by his wishes for the marriage once she has had time to grieve. Then he declares that, no need to wait, he is certain she will do as he says immediately. He proposes Wednesday as the wedding day, then suddenly asks what day it is. Paris says it is Monday. Capulet then says that the time is too short, and the wedding will be held on Thursday. He tells his wife to go to Juliet before she retires and inform her of the impending marriage.

ANALYSIS

The reason why Capulet decides that the wedding must take place so quickly is not explained. It might be that, with the added friction between the two households, it would be to Capulet's advantage to have Paris, a kinsman of the prince, on his side. In fact, during the conversation, Capulet often refers to Paris as "noble earl" or "my lord." Capulet later says that he wants to bring happiness to his daughter. However, it is obvious that both he and his wife want this marriage for social reasons and have no intentions of considering Juliet's feelings. They would not, in any case, understand a marriage based strictly on love.

Always an impetuous man, Capulet earlier told Paris at the feast that Juliet must agree to the match. Now he declares that his daughter will obey his wishes. Ironically Juliet is already married to Romeo. The scene also points to the powerlessness of women in Verona. This is further noted by the fact that Capulet had earlier declared that the marriage could not take place for two years. But now it will take place in a mere three days.

The many references to days and times in this scene speed up the action. They create a sense of urgency as the characters rush headlong to their inevitable fate. The tension between young and old, parents and children, is also noted. The Friar tries to calm Romeo's fears with quiet reasoning; Capulet decides Juliet's future without consulting her.

ACT III, SCENE 5

OVERVIEW

It is nearly dawn in Juliet's chamber, and the lovers must part. Once again their love flourishes in darkness. Juliet passionately tries to prolong Romeo's exit. She tells him that the bird they hear is a nightingale, a night bird, rather than the morning lark. She says that the light outside her chamber window is that of a meteor, not the sun.

Both lovers are well aware that if Romeo is found in Verona that morning, it will mean his death. Nonetheless Romeo listens to Juliet's pleas and declares that he will stay and face death rather than leave her. When she hears this, Juliet admits that the bird they heard was a lark and says Romeo must go.

The Nurse enters to say that Lady Capulet is coming. The lovers part, and Romeo leaves from the balcony (or window). As he does, Juliet looks down on him and thinks he looks pale, as though he were dead in the bottom of a tomb. Romeo says she also looks pale to him, but it is only their grief that makes them look that way. He leaves and Juliet responds to her mother's call.

Lady Capulet enters and thinks Juliet is tearful because of Tybalt's death. She tells her daughter that she wants only to see "the villain Romeo"

SIR FRANK DICKSEE'S 1884 OIL ON CANVAS PAINTING, DISPLAYED AT SOUTHHAMPTON CITY ART GALLERY, HAMPSHIRE, ENGLAND

dead. In a speech cleverly filled with puns, Juliet lets her mother think that she, too, wants Romeo dead, even while she is actually speaking of their love. But when Lady Capulet tells the young girl that her father has decided she will be married on Thursday, Juliet refuses: "I will not marry yet; and when I do, I swear,/It shall be Romeo—whom you know I hate—/Rather than Paris."

Capulet enters and becomes enraged at Juliet's refusal to marry Paris, calling her "young baggage" and "disobedient wretch." He says that if she does not agree to the marriage, she will never again look him in the face. Juliet pleads with her mother for help: "O sweet my mother, cast me not away!" Her mother replies, "Talk not to me, for I'll not speak a word." Both parents storm out of the chamber.

Juliet turns to the Nurse for counsel, but she is told only to marry Paris because Romeo's death is certain. Angered by the response, Juliet pretends to agree and says she is going to see the Friar to make her confession. Juliet leaves, knowing that she can never again rely on the Nurse for advice. She also realizes that if there is no other way out of this situation, she has the power to take her own life.

ANALYSIS

This scene once again shows that, despite the strength of their love, Romeo and Juliet cannot fight time. Before they part, Juliet tries to pretend that daylight is not coming and that it is still nighttime. She is also the more realistic of the two. When the morning light is obvious, Juliet says Romeo must leave. Despite this fact, Romeo is content to remain at her side. The vision that both of them have when they part, where they see one another pale as if they are at the bottom of a tomb, foreshadows what is to come, for this is the last moment they will spend alive together.

In this scene, Juliet grows to maturity. She dominates the conversation with her mother, who has no idea what she is talking about. She rejects

"NIGHT'S CANDLES ARE BURNT OUT"

her father's command to marry. She also realizes that the Nurse can no longer counsel her. However, while rejecting her father, Juliet also becomes aware of her own lack of power. Why does she not just leave her father's household and go to Romeo in Mantua? She cannot do this because she is aware of her place in society and her father's right to control her.

Lady Capulet is shown as brutally calculating, interested only in what will further the esteem of the household rather than in her daughter's welfare and feelings. Capulet himself is no longer the concerned father shown earlier when he spoke of Juliet's happiness. Now he emerges as an impulsive and even cruel man. His daughter has become a commodity to be sold for her value.

Even the loyal Nurse has turned against Juliet. Her solution is easy: Marry Paris because Romeo is doomed anyway. However, the Nurse's attitude is understandable to the audience. No matter how close the relationship is between the Nurse and Juliet, the older woman is a servant to the Capulets; she is not family.

When Juliet recognizes that the Nurse can no longer be trusted and decides instead to see the Friar, she leaves her childhood fully behind. If the Friar will not help her, Juliet will be totally alone. She knows that her choices are limited. She also knows that if she cannot live with Romeo, she will take her life rather than marry Paris: "If all else fail, myself have power to die."

ACT IV, SCENE 1

OVERVIEW

Paris speaks to the Friar in his cell, saying that Juliet's father has wisely decided they should marry on Thursday in order to end Juliet's sadness over Tybalt's death. The Friar silently wishes he himself did not know the true reason that the marriage should be delayed. Juliet enters. Although

Paris speaks to her lovingly, he is also somewhat arrogant in his manner, as though she is already his wife. Juliet's response is neutral, and she seems indifferent to him, although she does remark that they are not yet married.

Paris leaves, thinking Juliet has come to the Friar for confession. But with knife in hand, Juliet tells the Friar that she will kill herself rather than go through with the marriage: "O, bid me leap, rather than marry Paris,/From off the battlements of any tower." However, the sympathetic Friar has a plan. First, Juliet must outwardly agree to marry Paris. Then, on the night before the wedding, the Friar will give Juliet a sleeping potion. After she drinks it, she will appear to be dead: "When presently through all thy veins shall run,/A cold and drowsy humor. . . ./No warmth, no breath, shall testify thou livest." The Friar will then send a message to Romeo. After Juliet is laid to rest in the Capulet tomb, both Romeo and the Friar will be there when she awakens. Then the couple will go to Mantua to live together. Juliet agrees to this plan, and the Friar gives her a vial of the potion he has concocted.

ANALYSIS

The Friar is actually a wily character, although Shakespeare never presents him as such. Nor is he blamed for the tragedy that results from his plan. Once again the plan demonstrates the play's constantly intertwined themes of life and death, love and marriage. The Friar uses his knowledge of herbs to make up the potion that will put Juliet in a deathlike state. He is willing to help Juliet because of his own involvement in the situation. He has performed an illicit marriage and must now stop a bigamous one from occurring.

Paris's feelings for Juliet are never fully explained, and Shakespeare never allows the audience to understand his thoughts. Paris does assume, as do the Capulets, that Juliet's sadness is due to the death of Tybalt. He also assumes that she wants to marry him. He knows nothing of her relationship with Romeo. Paris is never unkind to Juliet, although he does act as though she is to be considered his property. He is presented, however, as having some real feelings for her. Even so, his kindness and his feelings for her terrify Juliet because she is already married and she does not love him.

Juliet has now matured fully. She has defied her father and is prepared to die if the Friar's plan does not work. She recognizes the danger: "Love give me strength!" But she is willing to be placed in a deathlike state in order to share her life with Romeo. This demonstrates not only her bravery, but the extent of her love for him.

JULIET (OLIVIA HUSSEY) REACHES FOR THE FRIAR'S SLEEPING POTION IN FRANCO ZEFFERELLI'S 1968 FILM.

"I DO SPY A KIND OF HOPE"

Although the idea of a deathlike sleeping potion may sound strange to modern ears, Shakespeare's audiences would have accepted it. Deep comas often could not be distinguished from death with the limited medical knowledge of the time. If someone looked dead, that was often taken as fact, without a doctor being called in. Being buried alive in such cases was an actual possibility. That is why when Juliet's parents see her in the deathlike trance, they simply accept the fact that she is dead and do not call a doctor to confirm it.

Again the concepts of love and death are united in this scene. Juliet must appear to die in order to live and share her love with Romeo. Shakespeare has reversed the natural human cycle of birth to death. Here, death comes first—in the form of Juliet's trancelike state. If the Friar's plan hadn't turned out so wrong, from that apparent death a new life for the lovers would have emerged.

ACT IV, SCENE 2

OVERVIEW

Juliet returns home from seeing the Friar to find her parents together, preparing for the wedding. To their great surprise, she suddenly regrets her earlier outburst and says, "Pardon, I beseech you!/Henceforward I am ever ruled by you." Then she quite cheerfully agrees to the marriage with Paris. In fact she is so cheerful that Capulet decides to move the ceremony up to Wednesday, the next day. Juliet agrees and tells the Nurse to find something for her to wear at the wedding. While she goes to her chamber (to drink the potion), Capulet runs off to tell Paris about the change in plans.

ANALYSIS

Here again time steps in to take over the fate of the lovers. Juliet's feigned cheerfulness and her apparent willingness to accept the marriage to Paris cause her father to change the wedding plans once again. The wedding is now scheduled for the next day. This gives Juliet time to take the potion, but it also means that the Friar now has less time to notify Romeo about the plan. As the audience will learn, that delay will prove fatal.

Capulet has now become totally authoritative and arrogant. He believes that his wishes are being obeyed, so he demands an earlier marriage date. This requires that the staff work through the night to prepare for the wedding. Capulet's authority over his wife and daughter reaches new heights in this scene. He orders his wife around, telling her to go help the Nurse with the wedding preparations. He refers to his daughter as "peevish self-willed harlotry." He says he will stay up all night and take charge of the plans: "I'll not to bed tonight; let me alone."

The difference between Juliet and her mother is especially striking here. Lady Capulet is shown as without power or respect and completely under the domination of her husband. But Juliet has taken control of her own life. While the household is in a frenzy over wedding preparations, she calmly retires to her chamber to take a potion that will put her in a deathlike state. She has removed herself from her surroundings. She has placed her trust in the Friar and his plan, and her devotion to Romeo is absolute.

ACT IV, SCENE 3

OVERVIEW

In her chamber, Juliet tells the Nurse and then her mother that she wishes to spend the night by herself. Thinking she needs time alone before the marriage, they depart. Her mother says, "Get thee to bed, and rest; for thou hast need." Now left alone and clutching the vial of sleeping potion, Juliet is overtaken by fright:

> WHAT IF IT BE A POISON WHICH THE FRIAR
> SUBTLY HATH MINISTERED TO HAVE ME DEAD,
> LEST IN THIS MARRIAGE HE SHOULD BE DISHONORED
> BECAUSE HE MARRIED ME BEFORE TO ROMEO?

Then, she imagines herself buried alive in a tomb:

> HOW IF, WHEN I AM LAID INTO THE TOMB,
> I WAKE BEFORE THE TIME THAT ROMEO
> COME TO REDEEM ME? THERE'S A FEARFUL POINT!

For a moment, the frightened thoughts continue. What if the Friar cannot be trusted? What if Romeo does not arrive on time? Suddenly she sees the ghost of Tybalt searching for Romeo. She weakens. However, the moment passes. She tells Tybalt's ghost to stop its search. She will be with Romeo: "Romeo, I come! This do I drink to thee." A resolute, mature Juliet drinks the potion.

ANALYSIS

The newfound strength of young Juliet reaches its climax. She understands the dangers facing her and the horrible consequences that could follow. But after an understandable moment of questioning, she accepts responsibility for her actions. She must trust the Friar. However, she also decides that if his plan fails and she does not go into a deathlike trance, she will be in charge of her life. To that end she places a dagger by her side before she drinks the potion. Previously Juliet has mainly just reacted to those around her. She waited for Romeo to name the time of their marriage. She consented to her father's wishes. She trusted the Friar to come up with a plan. Now, no longer a child, she is a woman and a wife who will decide her own fate.

ACT IV, SCENE 4

OVERVIEW

It is early morning and the Capulet household is still astir with wedding preparations. Lord Capulet has not yet been to bed, and he bustles around giving orders and shouting, "Make haste, make haste." The servants are dizzy with excitement. As daybreak approaches, he hears music. It signals that a group of musicians and Paris are on the way. Capulet tells the Nurse to get Juliet: "Go waken Juliet; go and trim her up." As the scene ends, Capulet says, "The bridegroom he is come already."

ANALYSIS

Capulet's last words are ironic, because Juliet already has a bridegroom, and it is not Paris. The frenzied atmosphere in the household contrasts sharply with the still body of Juliet, who lies in her bedchamber, apparently dead.

ACT IV, SCENE 5

OVERVIEW

The Nurse attempts to wake Juliet and finds her apparently dead. She screams for Capulet and Lady Capulet: "Alas, alas! Help, help! My lady's dead!" The two come immediately and all three despair over Juliet's lifeless body. Shortly after, the Friar and Paris arrive, as do the musicians for the wedding. The Friar asks if the bride is ready for the church service (knowing full well she is not), and Capulet informs them that Juliet is dead: "Death is my son-in-law."

The Friar joins in the sorrow, but tries to calm them all by saying that Juliet is now in a better place. After much moaning, the Friar takes charge and asks everyone to "follow this fair corse unto her grave." Everyone leaves except the Nurse and the musicians. Peter the servant enters and asks the musicians to play a joyful tune to make him feel better. The musicians are aghast because they feel such a request is inappropriate under the circumstances. There is some verbal sparring back and forth, and Peter leaves. The musicians, however, decide to wait until everyone returns so that they might get the lunch they were promised.

ANALYSIS

Once again the Nurse's view of love and marriage turns to the sexual. As she goes to awaken Juliet, she says that the next night, "You shall rest but little." The audience, meanwhile, knows what the Nurse is soon to discover.

Paris's feelings for Juliet are shown here by his grief at her supposed death: "Have I thought long to see this morning's face,/And doth it give me such a sight as this?" His words seem to indicate a sense of personal loss rather than mere disappointment over losing entry into a prominent family. The reactions of the Capulets also demonstrate genuine feelings for their daughter. Capulet speaks his most eloquent lines in the play when he says, "Death lies on her like an untimely frost/Upon the sweetest flower of all the field." It might also be argued that some of the Capulets' distress stems from the fact that they have lost the well-positioned Paris as a son-in-law. Capulet also describes Juliet's death in sexual terms, saying that death has taken her virginity: "There she lies,/Flower as she was, deflowered by him."

The scene between Peter and the musicians is sometimes dropped from productions of *Romeo and Juliet* because it seems out of place in the tragedy of the moment. However, some say it is legitimate comic relief, since what follows in the next act is the ultimate tragedy. Others say it indicates that not everyone feels this tragic sense. At first the musicians argue with Peter that playing a tune would be unseemly following Juliet's death. But it is soon obvious that what they are concerned about is the fact that they missed out on a job and a free lunch: "Come, we'll in here, tarry for the mourners, and stay dinner."

ACT V, SCENE 1

OVERVIEW

Although he is in banishment, Romeo is joyful when he awakens on Wednesday morning in Mantua. He just had a dream in which Juliet discovered his dead body and her kiss brought him back to life. Then Balthasar, Romeo's trusted servant, enters and Romeo is happy to see him because he thinks the servant brings news that the Friar has told people in Verona about their marriage. "How fares my Juliet?" he says. "That I ask again,/For nothing can be ill if she be well." Balthasar responds with the terrible news that Juliet is dead. In a rage against fate, Romeo shouts, "I defy you, stars!"

Romeo says that he will return to Verona that evening. Then he suddenly thinks to ask Balthasar if there is a message from Friar Lawrence, but the servant says there is not. Balthasar leaves to hire horses for the return journey.

Romeo now decides that he will kill himself in order to be with his beloved. In fact he will lie with Juliet that very evening. He goes to an apothecary (pharmacist) to get a vial of poison. The apothecary, however, refuses to sell it to him, saying that Mantua executes people who sell poison. Romeo can see that the man is obviously poor, so he offers the apothecary a large sum of money. The man then sells him the vial, which he guarantees will cause death: "Put this in any liquid thing you will/And drink it off, and if you had the strength/Of twenty men, it would dispatch you straight." With the poison in hand, Romeo is ready to return to Verona to kill himself at Juliet's tomb.

ANALYSIS

Fate now takes charge of the young lovers. Nothing can stop it. There is an outbreak of plague in the city. The Friar's messenger is forced into quarantine and cannot deliver the message about Juliet still being alive before Romeo leaves for Verona. Ironically Balthasar *was* able to deliver the false message of Juliet's death. Balthasar arrives on the scene wearing boots, which, to Elizabethan audiences, was a signal of bad tidings.

The character of Romeo changes in this scene. In many instances earlier he raged against fate. Now his reaction to the terrible news of Juliet's death is the decision to take command of his life. He will join his beloved in death. The haste with which he makes this decision to die is also one of many quick reactions—for instance, Romeo's quickly fighting a duel after Mercutio's death, or Capulet's quickly moving up the wedding day—that seal the fate of the characters in this play.

Shakespeare uses the character of the apothecary to show how human traits play a part in the outcome of human events. The apothecary says he can't sell the poison because the law (society) says it is illegal. But when he is offered a large sum of money, he does sell the poison because the society that makes the law also makes him poor.

ACT V, SCENE 2

OVERVIEW

The scene takes place in Friar Lawrence's cell, where he speaks with Friar John, who was sent to deliver the message concerning the plan in which Juliet faked her death. Friar John explains that he was unable to leave a quarantined house and could not deliver the message. Not knowing that Romeo has been told that Juliet is dead, Friar Lawrence fears that he will not be at Juliet's tomb according to the original plan. In three hours, Juliet will awaken. Someone must be there to rescue her: "Poor living corse, closed in a dead man's tomb!" The Friar tells Friar John to get a crowbar and decides that he must rescue Juliet by himself, planning to keep her in his cell until Romeo arrives. He will send another message to Romeo in Mantua, explaining what has happened.

SHAKESPEARE EXPLAINED: ROMEO AND JULIET

Once again fate takes over the lives of the characters. There is a sense of desperation as Friar Lawrence realizes that Romeo has not received his letter. "Unhappy fortune," he cries, referring to the forces of fate. Now the Friar himself must take action. At this point only he can keep his plan from total destruction. But this same sense of fate now also spellbinds the audience, which realizes—as the characters do not—that both Romeo and Juliet will die.

OVERVIEW

It is night in the churchyard and Paris enters with a servant, whom he immediately sends off to keep watch under a yew tree. Then Paris begins to spread flowers on Juliet's grave. When he hears his page's signal, he moves off and hides in the darkness. Romeo and Balthasar enter. Romeo carries a crowbar. He tells Balthasar that he is going to open the tomb in order to retrieve a ring that he had given to Juliet:

> WHY I DESCEND INTO THIS BED OF DEATH
> IS PARTLY TO BEHOLD MY LADY'S FACE,
> BUT CHIEFLY TO TAKE THENCE FROM HER DEAD FINGER
> A PRECIOUS RING, A RING THAT I MUST USE
> IN DEAR EMPLOYMENT.

Romeo also tells Balthasar to leave and to deliver a letter he has written to his father Montague in the morning.

Balthasar retreats as ordered. However, he stays nearby because he has some doubts about what Romeo is up to: "His looks I fear, and his intents I doubt."

Now Romeo opens Juliet's tomb. Paris, who is watching from his hiding place, recognizes Romeo as Tybalt's killer. Since Paris believes that Juliet died from grief over Tybalt's death, he marks Romeo as Juliet's killer as well. But why has Romeo returned from banishment to visit the Capulet tomb? Paris reasons that Romeo's hatred toward the Capulets is so great that he is willing to dishonor their gravesite. Enraged, Paris leaps out from his hiding place: "Obey, and go with me; for thou must die."

Romeo tries to stop the attack: "Good gentle youth, tempt not a desperate man." But Paris will not be turned away. The two men draw their swords as Paris's servant, observing from the darkness, runs off to find the watchman. In the fight, Paris is mortally wounded by Romeo. As he dies, he asks Romeo to be merciful and put his body in the tomb with Juliet.

Romeo agrees and places Paris in the tomb. As he does so, he looks at Juliet's body and wonders how she can look so beautiful in death: "Ah, dear Juliet,/Why art thou yet so fair?" He tells her that he has come to spend eternity with her. Romeo drinks the poison and says, "Thus with a kiss I die."

Friar Lawrence enters the graveyard carrying a crowbar, spade, and lantern. He meets Balthasar, who tells him that Romeo must be in the tomb. Balthasar says he fell asleep in his hiding place but had a dream that Romeo had a fight with someone. The Friar enters the tomb and finds the bodies of Paris and Romeo. As he is lamenting this tragedy, Juliet rises and says, "Where is my lord?" she asks. "Where is my Romeo?"

The Friar tells her that both Paris and Romeo are dead and that he fears the watch is coming. She must leave immediately. But when Juliet says she will not go, the Friar leaves without her. Alone, Juliet sees the vial of poison that Romeo drank. Thinking the poison might also kill her, she kisses Romeo. Now the watchmen and Paris's servant enter. As they approach, she quickly takes Romeo's dagger from its sheath and stabs herself. Juliet falls and dies.

There is much excitement as the watchmen view the bodies and also find the Friar and Balthasar nearby. Prince Escalus enters, followed by the Capulets and then Montague. He says that Lady Montague has died from grief over her son's banishment. The Capulets and Montague view the dead bodies of their children. The prince asks the Friar what has happened, and Friar Lawrence recounts the story of the secret marriage and the plan that failed. Balthasar gives the letter written by Romeo to the prince; this backs up the Friar's story.

The prince turns to Capulet and Montague, blaming them for the tragedy: "See what a scourge is laid upon your hate." Thus rebuked, Capulet and Montague shake hands. They vow to build gold statues of their lost children and to end the feud.

JULIET (CLAIRE DANES) LIES IN THE CAPULET TOMB IN THE 1996 MOVIE, ROMEO + JULIET.

The words of the prince end the tragedy: "For never was a story of more woe/Than this of Juliet and her Romeo."

ANALYSIS

It is ironic that the feud ends. By their deaths, Romeo and Juliet created the very world in which they would have been allowed to live and love. The audience senses this tragedy. The two young people become the symbols of true love because they were willing to sacrifice everything—even their lives—for that love. The lives of Romeo and Juliet are immortalized, but immortality seems empty because their triumph comes only in death. Their tragedy is that, in order to preserve their love, they must choose death.

It is interesting that the possibility of suicide is mentioned throughout the play. The love between Romeo and Juliet is intense. If it cannot be fulfilled, then they believe the only alternative is death, for neither can live without the other. At various times, both Romeo and Juliet express the feeling that if they cannot have their love, they are willing to die for it.

Appropriately the last scene takes place in the darkness. The two lovers have spent nearly all their time together in the dark. Now they will spend eternity there together.

THE SUN, FOR SORROW, WILL NOT SHOW HIS HEAD

LIST OF CHARACTERS

Romeo: Montague son and protagonist of the play.

Juliet: Daughter of the aristocratic Capulets and protagonist of the play.

Friar Lawrence: Romeo's confessor and adviser to the lovers.

Nurse: Juliet's confidante, who serves as a messenger between the lovers.

Mercutio: Romeo's friend and the defender of his honor.

Benvolio: Montague's nephew, who is a peacemaker.

Tybalt: Juliet's cousin, who challenges Romeo.

Capulet: Juliet's harsh and quick-tempered father.

Lady Capulet: Juliet's ineffectual mother.

Count Paris: A young nobleman who hopes to marry Juliet.

Escalus: Prince of Verona and kinsman of Mercutio and Paris.

Montague: Romeo's father and Capulet's enemy.

Lady Montague: Romeo's peace-seeking mother.

Balthasar: Romeo's servant and friend.

Apothecary: A poverty-stricken pharmacist. Desperate for money, the apothecary sells the illegal poison to Romeo.

Friar John: A Franciscan priest whom Friar Lawrence sends to deliver the message to Mantua that will tell Romeo about the sleeping potion.

ANALYSIS OF MAJOR CHARACTERS

ROMEO

Such is the depth of Romeo's feelings for Juliet that his name has become synonymous with *lover*. At first glance he appears to be a young man who is more in love with love than with any actual person. His passion-filled longings for the indifferent Rosaline seem juvenile. If he is not riding a cloud of euphoria, he is in the depths of total despair. Yet, immediately upon his meeting with Juliet, all thoughts of Rosaline vanish. From that moment on, Romeo's feelings for Juliet grow into an intense and profound passion. Even his speech matures, from the agonizing and exaggerated references to physical beauty he uses to discuss Rosaline to what are generally regarded as some of the most beautiful descriptions of love ever written.

Moderation is not a word in Romeo's vocabulary. Intelligent and quick-witted, he acts upon his emotions, a trait that, throughout the play, contributes to the tragic fate of the young lovers. He sneaks into the forbidden Capulet garden to catch a glimpse of his love. He refuses to fight Tybalt because they are now related through marriage. But when he places his love for Juliet over concern for his friend, Mercutio is killed. That compels Romeo to fight—and kill—Tybalt to avenge Mercutio's death. When he is banished from Verona, Romeo wails on the floor of the Friar's cell and halfheartedly tries to commit suicide. But when the Friar devises a plan, Romeo becomes calm and rational. And when he is told of Juliet's supposed death, he does not wail but calmly resolves to end his life in order to be with her.

In this great tragedy, both Romeo and Juliet, despite their ages, are not seen as overemotional adolescents. Instead, they become victims of fate, two people who have reached a level of passionate love that overshadows all else, even as it leads to their deaths. Although *Romeo and Juliet* may be a tragedy, it is above all a love story. It is a mature Romeo who grants the last wish of Paris to be placed near Juliet's grave. And it is a mature Romeo who takes poison because he cannot live without Juliet.

JULIET

The emphasis throughout the play is on Juliet's youth. Not yet fourteen years old, she stands between adolescence and maturity. However, during the course of the play, this innocent child turns into a responsible adult who takes control of her own destiny. As the play opens, Juliet is seen as an obedient girl who respects the wishes of her parents. When her mother says that Paris wishes to marry her, Juliet responds rather childishly by saying that she will see if she can love him. She is uncomfortable in any discussion of sex, as seen in her embarrassment when the Nurse tells a sexual joke. However, the strength of her character emerges in that scene with her mother and the Nurse.

After meeting Romeo at the feast, Juliet's first steps toward maturity begin. She is immediately willing to defy her parents, and she will even go so far as to marry him in secret. When Romeo is banished for killing Tybalt, Juliet is not blinded by love. She makes a rational decision that her loyalty must be toward her lover and husband. In so doing, she cuts all of the ties that bind her to her family and the Nurse. Her growing strength is further shown in Act IV, when she agrees to swallow a potion rather than enter into a bigamous marriage with Paris. Her decision to take her own life when she awakens to find that Romeo has died stems from the strength of her love for him. Her own suicide is a test of her resolve, in that she is able to stab herself with a dagger. This growth from a naïve and obedient child into a woman of strength and determination establishes Juliet as a confident character who becomes a tragic heroine.

FRIAR LAWRENCE

The audience may all too quickly dismiss Friar Lawrence as a minor character in the play. He is a kindhearted cleric, trusted by those around him, adviser to both Romeo and Juliet, and the play's only religious figure. Yet it is the Friar who is responsible for the tragic developments that take place. It is his schemes and plans that move the action along. Although he means well, his actions lead to the tragedy that ensues.

At first the Friar is not convinced of Romeo's feelings for Juliet, judging that the young man has been too hasty in declaring his devotion. However, he soon agrees to the marriage, mainly because he hopes the union will end the rift between the houses of Montague and Capulet. Thus the Friar's role becomes one of peacemaker. He does not yet believe that Romeo and Juliet are in love, but he sanctions the marriage because he hopes it will bring peace.

The Friar's somewhat mystical knowledge of plants is never fully explained, and seems unusual for a Catholic cleric. But this knowledge plays an important role in the events that follow. When the Friar comes up with the plan to give Juliet a potion, he is attempting to help the young lovers. But he is also trying to correct his mistakes. He has married the two; he cannot, as a religious man, sanction Juliet's double marriage to Paris. So he devises the plan to bring about her apparent death and subsequent revival.

In the scene where Juliet is discovered and presumed dead, the Friar shows himself capable of dishonesty. He hurries the families to accept the false death and complete the burial, using the justification that it is God's will. Yet, at the end, the Friar acts in a way that has little to do with God and religion; he runs from the tomb, leaving behind the drugged Juliet.

Friar Lawrence is a religious man, a well-meaning and kind man. He is also a person who is capable of making the wrong choices for the right reasons. Like all the other characters in the play, he succumbs to the ultimate tragedy. However, more than most, it is the Friar who helps bring about the tragedy.

NURSE

The role of the Nurse is important in two respects: As the play begins, she is a confidante for Juliet, and as the action progresses, she becomes the go-between for the lovers. She is also the only character besides the Friar who knows about the marriage between Romeo and Juliet. The Nurse is sometimes seen as a comic foil to Juliet; that is, she is someone who brings out the main qualities of another character.

The contrast between the Nurse and Juliet is striking. The older woman is coarse, speaking with many bawdy references to the physical side of love. She loves Juliet and regards her as a daughter, but she has no understanding of the intense spiritual feeling between her young charge and Romeo. The relationship between the two women keeps the focus on Juliet's age. The Nurse is old and constantly complains about her physical ailments. But her sexual remarks and ongoing patter introduce a feeling of lightheartedness within the tragedy of the play.

As the play opens, the Nurse is seen as Juliet's close confidante. She becomes a conspirator when Juliet confides her love for Romeo and her plan to marry him. The Nurse wants only happiness for the young girl. But when Romeo kills Tybalt and is banished, the Nurse sees trouble ahead. Therefore she advises Juliet to forget about Romeo and marry Paris, even though she is aware that Juliet is already married. By suggesting a false marriage, the Nurse loses Juliet's trust. Juliet now turns to the Friar for advice, and the Nurse is no longer included in her plans.

Like the Friar, the Nurse is a central character in moving along the action of the play. She is the main messenger. She is the one who identifies Romeo and Juliet at the feast. She carries messages between the two regarding their marriage. She brings the news to Juliet that Romeo has killed Tybalt and has been banished. She arranges for the wedding night. Finally, she tells Juliet to marry Paris and loses her role as confidante.

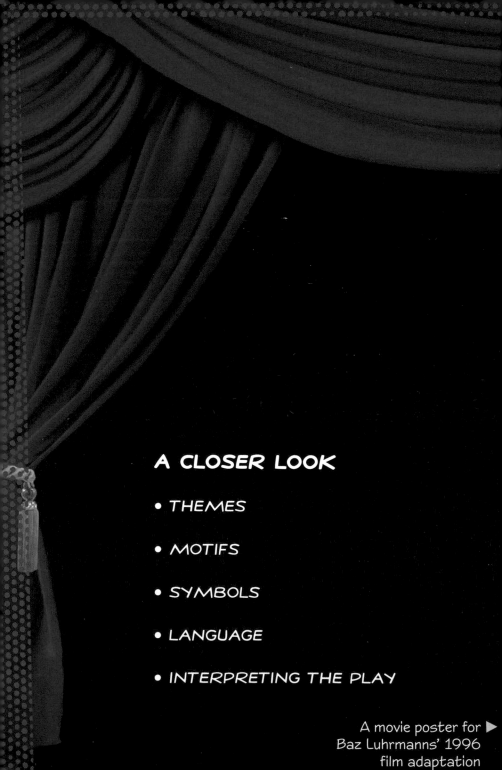

A CLOSER LOOK

- THEMES

- MOTIFS

- SYMBOLS

- LANGUAGE

- INTERPRETING THE PLAY

A movie poster for ▶
Baz Luhrmanns' 1996
film adaptation

LEONARDO DiCAPRIO CLAIRE DANES

WILLIAM SHAKESPEARE'S
ROMEO + JULIET

The greatest love story the world has ever known.

CHAPTER THREE

A Closer Look

THEMES

THE POWERFUL NATURE OF LOVE

The powerful nature of love and its consequences are evident throughout *Romeo and Juliet*. It is the most famous love story in English literature. But such love is not for the faint of heart. As Shakespeare describes it, the love that develops between Romeo and Juliet is all-powerful, even brutal. It is an overwhelming emotion that leads these young people to battle anything that stands in their way, even if that battle ends in their own destruction. Love makes them defy the normal boundaries of their world.

Romeo leaves his friends after the feast (Act II, Scene 1) to jump over the wall of the Capulets' orchard and catch a glimpse of Juliet:

> CAN I GO FORWARD WHEN MY HEART IS HERE?
> TURN BACK, DULL EARTH, AND FIND THY CENTER OUT.

Romeo tells his body (dull earth) to find Juliet (his heart, or center). He is also, in a sense, leaving his friends to start a new life with Juliet.

Juliet defies her father by secretly marrying Romeo and angers her father when she appears reluctant about a union with Paris. Romeo defies authority by breaking his exile and returning to Verona when Balthasar brings him news of Juliet's supposed death.

Shakespeare explores the different kinds of love in this play. There is love based on sexual pleasure. The Nurse speaks of this type of love, as does Mercutio, who talks of Romeo's despair over Rosaline. There is the so-called love that is actually infatuation, demonstrated by Romeo's great torment over the unfeeling Rosaline. He is in love with the idea and the passion of love.

> SHE IS TOO FAIR, TOO WISE, WISELY TOO FAIR,
> TO MERIT BLISS BY MAKING ME DESPAIR.
> SHE HATH FORSWORN TO LOVE, AND IN THAT VOW
> DO I LIVE DEAD THAT LIVE TO TELL IT NOW. 1.1

There is the love that may come about because of circumstances. Paris is, in today's language, "a good catch" for the Capulet family, and he does exhibit a kind of ownership over Juliet as the play progresses. However, one also gets the sense that he does have feelings for her, especially at the end, as he is mortally wounded.

> O, I AM SLAIN! IF THOU BE MERCIFUL,
> OPEN THE TOMB, LAY ME WITH JULIET. V.3

And there is the love that is instantaneous and overwhelming between Romeo and Juliet, what we often call true love. Beyond just a feeling, this love produces a willingness to do anything to obtain and keep it—even if to do so means death. This all-encompassing passion, coupled with the other main themes of the play, leads to its tragic conclusion.

HATE VERSUS LOVE

Love cannot exist without the theme of hate in *Romeo and Juliet*. Both love and hate determine the fate of the characters. The love between Romeo and Juliet is matched in power by the hatred between their two families. Interestingly the cause of the bitter feud is never explained; audiences are just supposed to accept that such hatred does exist and has existed for some time. Presumably, had their family differences been solved earlier, the tragedy of Romeo and Juliet would never have taken place.

Hate begins the trouble for the two lovers when Tybalt sees Romeo at the feast and remarks to his uncle:

> THIS IS A MONTAGUE, OUR FOE,
> A VILLAIN THAT IS HITHER COME IN SPITE
> TO SCORN AT OUR SOLEMNITY THIS NIGHT. I.5

Tybalt later sees Romeo on the street and insults him. When Romeo refuses to fight and Mercutio fights and dies, Romeo feels that he must fight Tybalt, which results in his banishment.

Even Juliet is affected by the atmosphere of hate that surrounds everyone. When her cousin Tybalt is killed by Romeo, she experiences a moment of doubt about her lover:

> ROMEO, THE LOVE I BEAR THEE CAN AFFORD
> NO BETTER TERM THAN THIS: THOU ART A VILLAIN.
> JUST OPPOSITE TO WHAT THOU JUSTLY SEEM'ST, A
> DAMNED SAINT, AN HONORABLE VILLAIN!. III.2

But when the Nurse speaks against Romeo, Juliet is quick to defend him:

> BLISTERED BE THY TONGUE FOR SUCH A WISH!
> HE WAS NOT BORN TO SHAME.
> UPON HIS BROW SHAME IS ASHAMED TO SIT III.2

Hate affects not only the main characters of the play, but also all of the supporting cast. The hatred between Montague and Capulet household servants leads to street brawls and more bloodshed between the two factions. It is as forceful as the power of love in moving the action of the play.

THE CERTAINTY OF FATE

The certainty of fate powerfully underlines all of the action in *Romeo and Juliet*. As the play opens, the Chorus speaks of "star-cross'd lovers." Their destinies are controlled by the stars, something that the characters themselves understand and accept. There is no escape. At the false news of Juliet's death, Romeo cries, "Then I defy you, stars" (Act V, Scene 1). He is acknowledging that their love is opposed by destiny, or fate.

After reading *Romeo and Juliet*, it is perhaps easy to blame everything that happens on bad luck. What if Tybalt hadn't recognized Romeo at the feast? What if Romeo hadn't met Tybalt on the street and refused to fight? What if Mercutio hadn't been so hot-tempered? What if there wasn't an epidemic of plague at the time? What if the letter to Romeo in Mantua had been delivered? What if Romeo had waited a few more minutes before he drank the poison? But there are no "what ifs" to this story; fate has taken control.

Especially in Elizabethan times, the idea of fate played an important role in people's lives. Many believed it was unchangeable. Certain circumstances occur throughout the play and lead to certain outcomes. Unfortunately for Romeo and Juliet, they each fall in love with a member of the bitterly opposed family. The Friar's well-meaning plan to give Juliet a potion and then unite the lovers goes wrong because of the plague that prevents the message from being delivered to Romeo. Fate interferes with the timing at Juliet's grave, when Romeo takes poison and dies only moments before Juliet awakens.

However inevitable fate is to Shakespeare, it can also be seen as a force that, while influencing human decisions, does not control them completely. Human personalities and weaknesses also play a role. Is fate the ultimate power, or do things happen because humans cause them to happen? Fate has the power to cause many of the events in *Romeo and Juliet*, yet it can also be seen as not completely in control of the outcome.

In Act III, Scene 1, Romeo bemoans the death of his friend Mercutio and blames fate:

> THIS DAY'S BLACK FATE ON MORE DAYS DOTH DEPEND;
> THIS BUT BEGINS THE WOE OTHERS MUST END.

But when Tybalt enters and feels no remorse at Mercutio's death, Romeo makes a choice. He decides that one of them must die to avenge Mercutio: "Either thou or I, or both, must go with him." When the two fight and Tybalt dies, Romeo, who cannot accept what he has done, reverts to fate once again: "O, I am fortune's fool!"

The final terrible hand of fate occurs at the end of the play when Juliet wakes and compounds Romeo's death by taking her own life. But just as she is gaining consciousness, the Friar leaves her alone because he hears the watch coming: "Come, go, good Juliet. I dare no longer stay" (Act V, Scene 3). Had he stayed with her, Juliet's death might have been prevented. The consequences of fate may be unalterable in *Romeo and Juliet*, but they are also influenced by human decisions and weaknesses.

MOTIFS

Two important motifs in *Romeo and Juliet* are the imagery of light and dark, and the use of time. The imagery of light and dark is one of the most consistent motifs in this play. Shakespeare uses light or its absence to contribute to the mood of the scenes. Because of their circumstances, the lovers must spend a good deal of their time together in the dark. But in their case and throughout the play, dark is not always evil and light does not always convey good.

Light and dark images recur often in conversations between Romeo and Juliet. When Romeo first sees Juliet at the feast, (Act I, Scene 5) he is moved to remark:

*O, SHE DOTH TEACH THE TORCHES TO BURN BRIGHT!
IT SEEMS SHE HANGS UPON THE CHEEK OF NIGHT. . . .*

But the most quoted use of light and dark imagery occurs in the famous Balcony Scene (Act II, Scene 2). After comparing Juliet to the sun, Romeo blurs day and night:

*THE BRIGHTNESS OF HER CHEEK WOULD
SHAME THOSE STARS
AS DAYLIGHT DOTH A LAMP. . . .*

Day and night is a vivid motif after the lovers spend their only night together (Act III, Scene 5). Now the light must be feared because it means they must part, sending Romeo into exile. They both try to keep the light from filling Juliet's chamber.

But when they cannot deny that morning is upon them, Juliet says, "O, now be gone! More light and light it grows." Romeo answers, "More light and light; more dark and dark our woes."

At the end of the play, the tragic consequences are entirely buried in the concept of the dark. Prince Escalus speaks these words (Act V, Scene 3) over the bodies of the young lovers:

> A GLOOMING PEACE THIS MORNING WITH IT BRINGS.
> THE SUN, FOR SORROW, WILL NOT SHOW HIS HEAD.

The important motif of time is evident everywhere in both the plot and the language of *Romeo and Juliet*. Shakespeare compresses the time span of the play into four days, compared to Brooke's poem, which covered about nine months. There are numerous references to time throughout, starting in the Prologue of Act I when the Chorus remarks,

> THE FEARFUL PASSAGE OF THEIR DEATH-MARKED LOVE,
> AND THE CONTINUANCE OF THEIR PARENTS' RAGE,
> WHICH, BUT THEIR CHILDREN'S END,
> NAUGHT COULD REMOVE,
> IS NOW THE TWO HOURS' TRAFFIC OF OUR STAGE. . . .

In addition, numerous characters frequently refer to time, citing specific hours or days of the week. In this way the audience is kept aware of how quickly time passes and how important it is to the story's development.

After their first meeting, the love between the two young people develops at an accelerated pace. Juliet recognizes this in Act II, Scene 2:

> ALTHOUGH I JOY IN THEE,
> I HAVE NO JOY OF THIS CONTRACT TONIGHT.
> IT IS TOO RASH, TOO UNADVISED, TOO SUDDEN,
> TOO LIKE LIGHTNING, WHICH DOTH CEASE TO BE
> ERE ONE CAN SAY IT LIGHTENS. SWEET, GOOD NIGHT.

After Romeo's banishment, time quickly becomes an enemy. Capulet speeds up Juliet's marriage date to Paris to ease what he thinks is her grief over the death of Tybalt. Even Paris remarks on the haste in Act III, Scene 4,

"These times of woe afford no times to woo." Because of the hasty marriage plans, Friar Lawrence makes up the potion as a way to unite the lovers. But in the end, time catches up with Romeo and Juliet, who must fight time if their love is to last forever. The fast pace eventually overtakes their lives. In their death, however, they defeat time and remain forever united in love.

Time is also connected to the motif of light and dark. There are many references throughout the play to night and day, the moon, sun, and stars. These references help create the sense of day and night. That is important because so much of the interplay between Romeo and Juliet must necessarily take place in the darkness.

SYMBOLS

In *Romeo and Juliet* poison is a symbol of death. The Friar makes a potion for Juliet that appears to bring on death. It does not do that, but it does, without intention, bring about Romeo's suicide. When Romeo buys poison from the apothecary (Act V, Scene 1), he says it is society's fault that the seller cannot make a decent living and so must break the law:

The apothecary replies, "My poverty but not my will consents."

In Shakespeare's play, poison is not evil of itself. As the Friar says in Act II, Scene 3, plants and herbs have special purposes in nature:

> O, MICKLE IS THE POWERFUL GRACE THAT LIES
> IN PLANTS, HERBS, STONES, AND THEIR TRUE QUALITIES;
> FOR NOUGHT SO VILE THAT ON THE EARTH DOTH LIVE
> BUT TO THE EARTH SOME SPECIAL GOOD DOTH GIVE.

These plants and herbs can be used for either good or bad. It is human intent that can turn a potion sold by the apothecary for healing into a poison that instead causes death. Shakespeare also shows poison to be a weapon that desperate people may use to solve their conflicts.

Foreshadowing is another strong symbol throughout the play. At various times the characters worry or are overcome by bad feelings. These feelings are symbols of the tragedy that awaits them. In this way, Shakespeare is telling the audience what it has known from the beginning—that Romeo and Juliet will die. But if, indeed, the audience knows from the outset that death lies ahead, why keep repeating it? The use of foreshadowing provides subtle clues and assures the audience of what will indeed happen. It also pulls the audience along as the plot thickens. For instance, Romeo has some bad feelings on his way to the Capulet feast (Act I, Scene 4):

> I FEAR, TOO EARLY; FOR MY MIND MISGIVES
> SOME CONSEQUENCE YET HANGING IN THE STARS. . . .

These bad feelings confirm what the audience knows; Romeo will now meet Juliet and begin the chain of events that leads to the tragedy. Each time a character shows worry or gloom, it is one more assurance of the inevitable ending. The audience may not like what is going to happen, but there is comfort in knowing what will take place before the characters do.

Foreshadowing occurs time and again throughout the play. In Act I, Scene 5, Tybalt has to obey his uncle and not attack Romeo at the feast. But the hot-tempered Tybalt does not forget what he sees as an insult:

> I WILL WITHDRAW. BUT THIS INTRUSION SHALL,
> NOW SEEMING SWEET, CONVERT TO BITT'REST GALL.

This tells the audience that Tybalt is going to cause trouble, which he eventually does, causing Mercutio's death and bringing on his own.

In that same scene, Juliet wants the Nurse to find out Romeo's name because she is afraid he is married:

> GO ASK HIS NAME. IF HE BE MARRIED,
> MY GRAVE IS LIKE TO BE MY WEDDING BED.

Juliet is saying that she already knows she will never marry if she cannot have Romeo. But the audience knows what will happen; her grave will indeed become her wedding bed.

In Act II, Scene 3, the Friar worries that Romeo is rushing too quickly into marriage: "Wisely and slow; they stumble that run fast." In Act IV, Scene 3, Juliet worries about the potion that the Friar has made for her: "What if it be a poison, which the friar/Subtly hath minister'd to have me dead." In scenes such as these, Shakespeare time and again tells the audience that fate continues to have the upper hand.

LANGUAGE

As in all his plays, Shakespeare used three forms of language in *Romeo and Juliet*: prose, rhymed verse, and blank verse.

Prose is ordinary speech, but it is not necessarily spoken only by the lower classes. There is no particular rhythm pattern and the lines don't have the same number of syllables. Shakespeare used prose for simple explanations of a situation, for scenes of everyday life, or just relaxed conversation. An example occurs in Act I, Scene 1, on a street in Verona. Two Capulet servants, Sampson and Gregory, see two servants from the hated Montague household approaching. They speak in prose:

> SAMPSON: LET US TAKE THE LAW OF OUR SIDES;
> LET THEM BEGIN.
> GREGORY: I WILL FROWN AS I PASS BY,
> AND LET THEM TAKE IT AS THEY LIST.
> SAMPSON. NAY, AS THEY DARE. I WILL BITE MY THUMB
> AT THEM, WHICH IS DISGRACE TO THEM IF THEY BEAR IT.

Shakespeare uses some lines of prose in many of the scenes throughout the play. The characters in Act II, Scene 4, and Act III, Scene 1, for instance, speak mainly in prose. An example is the Nurse's agitated conversation with Romeo when she is trying to arrange a meeting:

> NURSE: NOW, AFORE GOD, I AM SO VEXED
> THAT EVERY PART ABOUT ME QUIVERS.
> SCURVY KNAVE! PRAY YOU, SIR, A WORD:
> AND, AS I TOLD YOU, MY YOUNG LADY
> BID ME INQUIRE YOU OUT. WHAT SHE BID ME SAY,
> I WILL KEEP TO MYSELF. BUT
> FIRST LET ME TELL YE, IF YE SHOULD LEAD HER
> INTO A FOOL'S PARADISE, AS THEY
> SAY, IT WERE A VERY GROSS KIND OF BEHAVIOR, AS THEY
> SAY; FOR THE GENTLE-WOMAN IS YOUNG, AND THEREFORE, IF
> YOU SHOULD DEAL DOUBLE WITH HER, TRULY
> IT WERE AN ILL THING TO BE OFFERED TO ANY
> GENTLEWOMAN, AND VERY WEAK DEALING.

The Nurse's speech is also an example where the use of prose does indicate the lower class of the speaker, as well as its humorous effect.

Rhymed verse is usually in the form of two lines whose ending words rhyme with each other. For instance, referring to Rosaline, Romeo speaks this rhymed verse at the end of in Act I, Scene 2:

> I'LL GO ALONG, NO SUCH SIGHT TO BE SHOWN,
> BUT TO REJOICE IN SPLENDOR OF MINE OWN.

Disregarding the standard rules of prose, the first words of every line of verse are capitalized. Shakespeare often used rhymed verse in prologues and in passages that give advice or are very lyrical. Act II, Scene 3, contains only rhymed verse. In part of this passage, Friar Lawrence expresses his surprise at how quickly Romeo has turned his attention away from the fair Rosaline:

> HOLY SAINT FRANCIS! WHAT A CHANGE IS HERE!
> IS ROSALINE, THAT THOU DIDST LOVE SO DEAR,
> SO SOON FORSAKEN? YOUNG MEN'S LOVE THEN LIES
> NOT TRULY IN THEIR HEARTS, BUT IN THEIR EYES.
> JESU MARIA! WHAT A DEAL OF BRINE
> HATH WASHED THY SALLOW CHEEKS FOR ROSALINE!

The play also finishes (Act V, Scene 3) with two rhymed lines, called a rhyming couplet. They are spoken by Prince Escalus:

> FOR NEVER WAS A STORY OF MORE WOE
> THAN THIS OF JULIET AND HER ROMEO.

Blank verse refers to unrhymed iambic pentameter. That means most lines have ten syllables. They alternate between stressed and unstressed syllables. Like prose, the last words in the lines don't rhyme in any regular pattern. But you can tell blank verse from prose by reading it aloud. It has a regular pattern. Romeo's opening speech to Juliet in the famous Balcony Scene (Act II, Scene 2) is in blank verse, which begins: "But soft! What light through yonder window breaks?" You can also tell blank verse by looking at it. The first word in each line is capitalized, and not all the lines are the same length or fill the page. In Shakespeare's plays, blank verse is often used because it closely resembles the natural speaking patterns of English. It also marks great or passionate occasions. Many of Shakespeare's most famous speeches are written in blank verse.

Act III, Scene 4, contains only blank verse, as do Act IV, Scenes 3 and 4, and Act V, Scene 2. In the latter, Friar Lawrence finds out that Friar John was not able to deliver the message to Romeo about the potion Friar Lawrence gave to Juliet. Friar Lawrence is now faced with a problem:

> UNHAPPY FORTUNE! BY MY BROTHERHOOD,
> THE LETTER WAS NOT NICE BUT FULL OF CHARGE,
> OF DEAR IMPORT, AND THE NEGLECTING IT
> MAY DO MUCH DANGER. FRIAR JOHN, GO HENCE;
> GET ME AN IRON CROW AND BRING IT STRAIGHT
> UNTO MY CELL.

John replies that he will do so, and Friar Lawrence says:

> NOW MUST I GO TO THE MONUMENT ALONE.
> WITHIN THIS THREE HOURS WILL FAIR JULIET WAKE.
> SHE WILL BESHREW ME MUCH THAT ROMEO
> HATH HAD NO NOTICE OF THESE ACCIDENTS;
> BUT I WILL WRITE AGAIN TO MANTUA,
> AND KEEP HER AT MY CELL TILL ROMEO COME.
> POOR LIVING CORSE, CLOSED IN A DEAD MAN'S TOMB!

The language is one of the most compelling aspects of *Romeo and Juliet*. The characters jest and curse, scream at each other, and beat their chests in emotional anguish. Puns and witty sexual references abound. It is a splendid linguistic show.

IT IS THE EAST, AND JULIET IS THE SUN

This is probably the play's most famous and oft-quoted scene. Romeo stands below, looking up at Juliet on the balcony (or at the window). He speaks of his love and passion for her in what is often thought of as the epitome of romantic expression. Remember that this is blank verse and is meant to be read in a regular pattern. The speech is flowery even for that time, and full of symbols. These lines are to be read with the understanding that Shakespeare uses such methods to convey the extent of Romeo's feelings. After hearing the speech, the audience is aware that, for Romeo, this is nothing like his musings over the fair Rosaline; it is nothing like anything he has ever experienced. The very depth that this speech conveys is the underlying reason that both of the lovers are willing to—and do—die for their love. Without that understanding, the audience cannot comprehend the tragedy that ensues.

Romeo pours out his heart, first by comparing Juliet to the sunrise. He likens the window of her chamber to the eastern horizon at dawn:

BUT SOFT! WHAT LIGHT THROUGH YONDER WINDOW BREAKS?
IT IS THE EAST, AND JULIET IS THE SUN.

Romeo implores Juliet to appear at the window, telling her that the moon (actually the moon goddess Diana) is sad because Juliet's beauty is greater than hers, just as the sun's light is greater than that of the moon:

ARISE, FAIR SUN, AND KILL THE ENVIOUS MOON,
WHO IS ALREADY SICK AND PALE WITH GRIEF
THAT THOU, HER MAID, ART FAR MORE FAIR THAN SHE.

Romeo says that Juliet must no longer serve the moon goddess, who is jealous of her:

BE NOT HER MAID, SINCE SHE IS ENVIOUS;
HER VESTAL LIVERY IS BUT SICK AND GREEN,
AND NONE BUT FOOLS DO WEAR IT; CAST IT OFF.

And now, Juliet actually appears at the window, and Romeo is struck with her beauty:

IT IS MY LADY, O, IT IS MY LOVE!
O, THAT SHE KNEW SHE WERE!

Romeo cannot hear Juliet, but he talks himself into thinking she is talking to him:

SHE SPEAKS, YET SHE SAYS NOTHING. WHAT OF THAT?
HER EYE DISCOURSES; I WILL ANSWER IT.

Presumably he takes a step toward the window, then realizes she is unaware of his presence below:

I AM TOO BOLD; 'TIS NOT TO ME SHE SPEAKS.

So, once more, he returns to the imagery of light. He says that the two most beautiful stars in the heavens should ask the eyes of Juliet to fill in for them:

> TWO OF THE FAIREST STARS IN ALL THE HEAVEN,
> HAVING SOME BUSINESS, DO ENTREAT HER EYES
> TO TWINKLE IN THEIR SPHERES TILL THEY RETURN.
> WHAT IF HER EYES WERE THERE, THEY IN HER HEAD?

He continues to compare her beauty to nature's light, saying that her eyes could change night into day and make the birds sing:

> THE BRIGHTNESS OF HER CHEEK WOULD SHAME THOSE STARS
> AS DAYLIGHT DOTH A LAMP; HER EYES IN HEAVEN
> WOULD THROUGH THE AIRY REGION STREAM SO BRIGHT
> THAT BIRDS WOULD SING AND THINK IT WERE NOT NIGHT.

Then, like many young men in love, he becomes even more poetic and dazzled by Juliet's beauty:

> SEE HOW SHE LEANS HER CHEEK UPON HER HAND!
> O, THAT I WERE A GLOVE UPON THAT HAND,
> THAT I MIGHT TOUCH THAT CHEEK!

In the opening lines, Romeo calls Juliet the sun. Even the moon, often regarded as a symbol of feminine beauty, is envious of her. But none of these lines is meant to be taken literally. Romeo is well aware that Juliet is not the sun. He knows the moon is not jealous of her. But he uses these symbols of light and beauty to show that, for him, Juliet surpasses them all.

Note the use of comparisons throughout the speech. Besides comparing her to the sun and moon, he says Juliet's eyes are fairer than the stars in heaven. They are so fair that the brightness of her cheek outshines them, so fair that the birds think daylight has come.

INTERPRETING THE PLAY

HISTORICAL CONTEXT

Shakespeare probably wrote *Romeo and Juliet* in the early 1590s, although the exact date is unknown. In Act I, Scene 3, the Nurse talks of an earthquake: "'Tis since the earthquake now eleven years." There was an earthquake in England in 1580, which would put the writing at 1591. Most experts, however, think the play was written later.

Shakespeare acknowledges the plague in *Romeo and Juliet.* In fact it plays a large role in determining the fate of the lovers. Because of the plague quarantine, the message about Juliet and the potion never reaches Romeo. In Act V, Scene 2, Friar John tells Friar Lawrence that he could not get the message to Romeo because "Where the infectious pestilence did reign," the officials of the town "Sealed up the doors and would not let us forth." When Friar Lawrence then asks who was able to deliver the message, John replies:

> I COULD NOT SEND IT,—HERE IT IS AGAIN,—
> NOR GET A MESSENGER TO BRING IT THEE,
> SO FEARFUL WERE THEY OF INFECTION.

INFLUENCES OF *ROMEO AND JULIET*

Romeo and Juliet has been staged, performed, written about, sung about, imitated, modernized, and endlessly discussed. It is the world's ultimate love story. Its influence on all subsequent romantic literature is enormous. The words *Romeo* and *lover* mean the same thing in the English-speaking world. To call a young man "Romeo" indicates that he is highly attractive to the opposite sex. The actresses who played the female title role were known for wearing a "Juliet cap," a wedding headband that holds the veil. Both of the title characters have become symbols of romantic and passionate love, of young love, and of those who defy authority for a greater goal.

Along with *Hamlet, Romeo and Juliet* ranks as one of Shakespeare's most-performed plays. The London theaters were closed for a time by the Puritans in 1642 but reopened in 1660 when the monarchy was restored. Two years later, Henry Harris starred as Romeo, with Mary Saunderson playing Juliet. She was probably the first woman to play the role, as young boys had played the part until then. But there were all sorts of changes made to the play thereafter. Some versions changed the ending, so the young lovers did not die. Another had Juliet awaken just before Romeo died. Another changed the setting to ancient Rome, and some toned down Shakespeare's sexual language. It was not until 1845 that the original version returned to the stage in the U.S. and shortly afterward in England.

In 1935 the renowned English actors John Gielgud and Laurence Olivier played the roles of Romeo and Mercutio. After a six-week run, they exchanged parts. In 1986 the Royal Shakespeare Company set the play in present-day Verona. In this souped-up version, the feast becomes a rock party with drugs, the men fight with switchblades instead of swords, and Romeo dies not from a dagger but from a hypodermic needle.

Shakespeare's masterpiece also influenced the world of opera and ballet. Of the many operas based on the famous play, the best known is Charles Gounod's *Romeo et Juliette*, first performed in 1867. The 2004–2005 season of the Paris Opera Ballet included the classic love story, which featured the work of two other legends besides Shakespeare. This production used the choreography of the great ballet dancer Rudolf Nureyev. The Russian-born Nureyev, who died in 1993, had first choreographed *Romeo and Juliet* in 1977 for the London Festival Ballet.

Critics said his version more closely followed Shakespeare's story than most others do. The choreography was complemented by the masterful score of Romantic composer Sergei Prokofiev's version, which had debuted in 1938.

In addition, *Romeo and Juliet* is certainly no stranger to the silver screen, having been filmed numerous times, beginning in the silent era. The 1936 version received four Oscar nominations but has not stood the test of time, possibly because the stars Norma Shearer and Leslie Howard were much older than the original lovers. Franco Zeffirelli's 1968 film is an exciting and colorful version, and a good introduction to visualize the play. Regrettably, however, Zeffirelli spends most of the time on the first half of the tragedy, understating the importance of the development of Juliet's maturity. In this version, Romeo and Juliet are seventeen and fifteen, respectively. Baz Luhrmann directed a hip adaptation of the play in the 1996 film *Romeo + Juliet* starring Leonardo DiCaprio and Claire Danes. Set in the California suburb of Verona, the film's script retains Shakespeare's original dialogue.

The most famous musical adaptation in the Broadway theater (1957) and on film (1961) is *West Side Story*, with music by Leonard Bernstein and lyrics by Stephen Sondheim. In this updated retelling, the Montagues and Capulets become the Jets and the Sharks, rival gangs in Manhattan, and the ill-fated lovers are ex-Jet Tony and Maria, sister of the Puerto Rican gang leader. The Broadway run lasted 732 performances; the Hollywood version took ten Oscars, and a special award went to Jerome Robbins for choreography. Shakespeare lives on.

TONE

The tone of a play doesn't refer to *what* is said or done; it refers to *how*. Tone comes from language, symbols, diction, images, syntax (the rules of grammar), and allusion (references to a person, place, or event). In other

IN THE 1961 FILM *WEST SIDE STORY*, ADAPTED FROM SHAKESPEARE'S PLAY, THE JETS CLAIM THEIR TURF WITH A HIGH-ENERGY DANCE.

words, the tone of a play results from the play's many parts.

In *Romeo and Juliet,* there are obvious and dramatic changes of tone throughout the play. In Act II, Scene 2, for example, everything is romantic and hopeful as the lovers speak in the Capulet orchard. Romeo and Juliet express their love and desire to be together. The images of passionate and enduring love abound. But by the end of Act II, in Scene 6, there is an aura of encroaching doom. This is a short scene that ends with the lovers being married by the Friar. Even as he wishes to be married to Juliet, Romeo speaks of death, saying that not even death can take away the pleasure he feels in this marriage.

Almost immediately as the curtain opens on Act III, the tone of doom widens into an atmosphere of bursting tempers, sharp discourse, and sudden violence. When Tybalt asks to speak to a Capulet, Mercutio immediately responds with a threat: "And but one word with one of us? Couple it with something; make it a word and blow." The fiery Tybalt replies, "You shall find me apt enough to that, sir, an you will give me occasion." When Romeo refuses to draw his sword, the hot-tempered Mercutio immediately answers Tybalt's challenge: "Will you pluck your sword out of his pilcher by the ears? Make haste, lest mine be about your ears ere it be out." When Mercutio is wounded, his usual banter and wit sharply change: "Ask for me tomorrow, and you shall find me a grave man."

These and many other instances of tone differences throughout the play help move the action along. They are indicators of what lies ahead. With each clever shift in tone, the audience comes to realize that the circumstances surrounding the two lovers are about to change and nothing will stop the course of tragic events.

Chronology

1564   William Shakespeare is born on April 23 in Stratford-upon-Avon, England

1578–1582   Span of Shakespeare's "Lost Years," covering the time between leaving school and marrying Anne Hathaway of Stratford

1582   At age eighteen Shakespeare marries Anne Hathaway, age twenty-six, on November 28

1583   Susanna Shakespeare, William and Anne's first child, is born in May, six months after the wedding

1584   Birth of twins Hamnet and Judith Shakespeare

1585–1592   Shakespeare leaves his family in Stratford to become an actor and playwright in a London theater company

1587   Public beheading of Mary Queen of Scots

1593–94   The Bubonic (Black) Plague closes theaters in London

1594–96   As a leading playwright, Shakespeare creates some of his most popular work, including *A Midsummer Night's Dream* and *Romeo and Juliet*

1596   Hamnet Shakespeare dies in August at age eleven, possibly of plague

1596–97	*The Merchant of Venice* and *Henry IV, Part One* most likely are written
1599	The Globe Theater opens
1600	*Julius Caesar* is first performed at the Globe
1600–01	*Hamlet* is believed to have been written
1601–02	*Twelfth Night* is probably composed
1603	Queen Elizabeth dies; Scottish king James VI succeeds her and becomes England's James I
1604	Shakespeare pens *Othello*
1605	*Macbeth* is composed
1608–1610	London's theaters are forced to close when the plague returns and kills an estimated 33,000 people
1611	*The Tempest* is written
1613	The Globe Theater is destroyed by fire
1614	Reopening of the Globe
1616	Shakespeare dies on April 23
1623	Anne Hathaway, Shakespeare's widow, dies; a collection of Shakespeare's plays, known as the First Folio, is published

Source Notes

p. 40, par. 1, For a comparison between *Romeo and Juliet* and the poem by Arthur Brooke, see "How Romeus Became Romeo," http://www.amrep.org/articles/4_3a/romeus.html

p. 47, par. 1, View the modern city of Verona, including the street on which Juliet lived, in "Verona, Italy – City of Romance and Beauty," www.offbeattravel.com/verona.html

p. 51, par. 1, Shakespeare's introduction of Queen Mab, a fairy in Celtic folklore, sparked the interest of other authors. See: "Queen Mab," http://shakespeare.about.com.blmab.htm

p. 82, par. 2, The Worshipful Society of Apothecaries of London was incorporated on December 6, 1617, recognizing skills in dispensing medicines. It has been in its present building since 1666. The Society has licensed doctors since 1815 and grants eleven postgraduate degrees.

p. 96, par. 4, Duels may have been officially taboo in Shakespeare's time, but they were a common way to avenge an insult to one's honor. See: "The Duel," http://internetshakespeare.uvic.ca/Library/SLT/society/duels.html and "Life in Elizabethan England: Honor and Dueling," renaissance.duelingmodems.com/compendium/26.html

p. 99, par. 1, Light and dark were important motifs to Shakespeare. An interesting description of the actual lighting in which Shakespeare wrote, as well as his writing utensils, and the ways in which he prepared a manuscript are found in "How Shakespeare Prepared Manuscripts," http://www.cummingsstudyguides.net/xIllustrations.html

a Shakespeare Glossary

The student should not try to memorize these, but only refer to them as needed. We can never stress enough that the best way to learn Shakespeare's language is simply to *hear* it—to hear it spoken well by good actors. After all, small children master every language on earth through their ears, without studying dictionaries, and we should master Shakespeare, as much as possible, the same way.

addition —a name or title (knight, duke, duchess, king, etc.)
admire —to marvel
affect —to like or love; to be attracted to
an —if ("An I tell you that, I'll be hanged.")
approve —to prove or confirm
attend —to pay attention
belike —probably
beseech —to beg or request
betimes —soon; early
bondman —a slave
bootless —futile; useless; in vain
broil —a battle
charge —expense, responsibility; to command or accuse
clepe, clept —to name; named
common —of the common people; below the nobility
conceit —imagination
condition —social rank; quality
countenance —face; appearance; favor
cousin —a relative
cry you mercy —beg your pardon
curious —careful; attentive to detail
dear —expensive
discourse —to converse; conversation
discover —to reveal or uncover
dispatch —to speed or hurry; to send; to kill
doubt —to suspect

entreat —to beg or appeal

envy —to hate or resent; hatred; resentment

ere —before

ever, e'er —always

eyne —eyes

fain —gladly

fare —to eat; to prosper

favor —face, privilege

fellow —a peer or equal

filial —of a child toward its parent

fine —an end; in fine = in sum

fond —foolish

fool —a darling

genius —a good or evil spirit

gentle —well-bred; not common;

gentleman —one whose labor was done by servants (Note: to call someone a *gentleman* was not a mere compliment on his manners; it meant that he was above the common people.)

gentles —people of quality

get —to beget (a child)

go to —"go on"; "come off it"

go we —let us go

haply —perhaps

happily —by chance; fortunately

hard by —nearby

heavy —sad or serious

husbandry —thrift; economy

instant —immediate

kind— one's nature; species

knave— a villain; a poor man

lady— a woman of high social rank (Note: *lady* was not a synonym for *woman* or *polite woman*; it was not a compliment, but, like *gentleman*, simply a word referring to one's actual legal status in society.)

leave — permission; "take my leave" = depart (with permission)

lief, lieve —"I had as lief" = I would just as soon; I would rather

like —to please; "it likes me not" = it is disagreeable to me

livery —the uniform of a nobleman's servants; emblem
mark —notice; pay attention
morrow —morning
needs —necessarily
nice —too fussy or fastidious
owe —to own
passing —very
peculiar —individual; exclusive
privy —private; secret
proper —handsome; one's very own ("his proper son")
protest —to insist or declare
quite —completely
require —request
several —different, various;
severally —separately
sirrah —a term used to address social inferiors
sooth —truth
state —condition; social rank
still —always; persistently
success —result(s)
surfeit —fullness
touching —concerning; about; as for
translate —to transform
unfold —to disclose
villain —a low or evil person; originally, a peasant
voice —a vote; consent; approval
vouchsafe —to confide or grant
vulgar —common
want —to lack
weeds —clothing
what ho —"hello, there!"
wherefore —why
wit —intelligence; sanity
withal —moreover; nevertheless
without —outside
would —wish

Suggested Essay Topics

1. Discuss the ways in which the long-standing feud between the Montagues and Capulets helps bring about the tragedy of Romeo and Juliet.

2. How does the concept of masculine honor help bring about the deaths of both Mercutio and Tybalt?

3. Shakespeare portrays Romeo as an adolescent boy. Imagine the play staged in a modern setting. According to his actions, how old do you think Romeo should be and why? Would he act differently today? Why?

4. Do you think Juliet's father really loved her, or did he regard her mainly as a source of wealth and prestige for his family? Explain your answer.

5. Show instances throughout the play that indicate Juliet's growing maturity.

Testing Your Memory

1. Where is the play set?

   a) France; b) England; c) Italy; d) Scotland.

2. *Romeo and Juliet* belongs in which category of Shakespeare's works?

   a) histories; b) sonnets; c) comedies; d) tragedies.

3. Who introduces the play in the prologue of act 1?

   a) Romeo; b) the Chorus; c) Queen Mab; d) Juliet.

4. What word or phrase is often used throughout the play to describe the lovers?

   a) melancholy; b) devious; c) star-crossed; d) untrustworthy.

5. A sonnet, such as the one that opens the play, has how many lines?

   a) 14; b) 6; c) 8; d) 12.

6. Romeo is part of which family?

   a) Capulet; b) Montague; c) Mantua; d) Verona.

7. As the play opens, Romeo is in love with which beautiful lady?

   a) Rosaline; b) Juliet; c) Mercutio's sister; d) Tybalt's mother.

8. How old is Juliet?

   a) 21; b) 17; c) 16; d) 13.

9. Juliet's parents want her to marry which man?

   a) Paris; b) Escalus; c) Tybalt; d) Romeo.

10. Where does Romeo first see Juliet?

    a) at Friar Lawrence's; b) at Capulet's feast; c) at Mercutio's;
    d. on a street in Verona.

11. Why does Friar Lawrence agree to marry Romeo and Juliet?

    a) He is angry with Romeo's father; b) He is angry with Juliet's father;
    c) The bishop orders him to do so; d) He thinks their marriage might
    end the feud.

12. After his marriage to Juliet, Romeo becomes related to what man?

   a) Capulet; b) Mercutio; c) Tybalt; d) Peter.

13. Who kills Mercutio?

   a) Romeo; b) Benvolio; c) Capulet; d) Tybalt.

14. Who discovers the supposedly dead body of Juliet in her chamber?

   a) Lady Capulet; b) Capulet; c) Romeo; d) The Nurse.

15. Whom does Romeo kill before he dies?

   a) Paris; b) Capulet; c) Juliet; d) Sampson.

16. How does Romeo commit suicide?

   a) with his dagger; b) with a gun; c) with poison; d) by hanging himself.

17. How does Juliet die?

   a) She swallows poison; b) She jumps off a cliff; c) She stabs herself with Romeo's dagger; d) She stabs herself with her father's dagger.

18. The action of the play takes place over how many days?

   a) 3; b) 4; c) 7; d) 9.

19. How does Lady Montague react to Romeo's banishment?

   a) She dies of grief; b) She leaves Verona to be with him; c) She is happy; d) She divorces her husband.

20. Who speaks the last words in the play?

   a) Romeo; b) Juliet; c) Capulet; d) Escalus.

Answer Key

1. c; 2. d; 3. b; 4. c; 5. a; 6. b; 7. a; 8. d; 9. a; 10. b; 11. d; 12. c; 13. d; 14. d; 15. a; 16. c; 17. c; 18. b; 19. a; 20. d.

Further Information

BOOKS

Evans, G. Blakemore, ed. *Romeo and Juliet: The New Cambridge Shakespeare.* New York: Cambridge University Press, 2003.

Folger Shakespeare Library: *Romeo and Juliet.* New York: Washington Square Press, 2004.

Manga Shakespeare series: *Romeo and Juliet.* New York: Harry N. Abrams/Amulet, 2007.

Rosen, Michael. *Shakespeare: His Work and World.* Cambridge, MA: Candlewick Press, 2006.

Selfors, Suzanne. *Saving Juliet.* New York: Walker, 2008.

WEB SITES

http://absoluteshakespeare.com
Summaries of Shakespeare's plays, poems, sonnets, and his famous quotes

www.WestSideStory.com
Official site for fans, photos, and lyrics

http://www.williamshakespeare.info/site-map.htm
Shakespeare biography and history of the plague in Europe

FILMS

Romeo and Juliet (1968) with Leonard Whiting and Olivia Hussey. Called one of the best cinematic versions of the tragedy, narrated by Laurence Olivier.

Romeo and Juliet (1996) with Claire Danes and Leonardo DiCaprio. A '90s version of the tragic love story, set in Miami.

West Side Story (1961) starring Natalie Wood and Richard Beymer, choreography by Jerome Robbins. Updating Romeo and Juliet to New York City in the late 1950s, with the feud now between rival gangs.

AUDIO BOOK

Romeo and Juliet, BBC Audiobooks, with Douglas Henshall, Sophie Dahl, and Susannah York, length 3 hours, 2006.

RECORDINGS

Prokofiev: *Romeo and Juliet,* conductor Andre Previn, London Symphony Orchestra, 1996.

Bibliography

William Shakespeare

Bevington, David, ed. *Bringing Shakespeare Back to Life.* Naperville, IL: Sourcebooks, 2005.

Bloom, Harold, ed. *William Shakespeare The Tragedies: Modern Critical Views.* New York: Chelsea, 1985.

Romeo and Juliet

Fallon, Robert Thomas. *A Theatergoer's Guide to Shakespeare's Characters.* Chicago: Dee, 2004.

McLeish, Kenneth. *Shakespeare's Characters.* Studio City, CA: Players Press, 1992.

Shakespeare, William. *Romeo and Juliet.* New York: Houghton Mifflin, 1966.

Index

Page numbers in **boldface** are illustrations.

About the Author

A former children's book editor and U.S. Navy journalist, Corinne J. Naden has written more than ninety books for children and young adults. She lives in Tarrytown, New York.